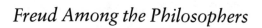
Freud Among the Philosophers

DONALD LEVY

Freud Among the Philosophers

. . . .

THE PSYCHOANALYTIC UNCONSCIOUS AND ITS PHILOSOPHICAL CRITICS

Yale University Press
New Haven & London

Designed by Betty Ng. Set in Sabon type by Keystone Typesetting, Inc., Orwigsburg, Pennsylvania. Printed in the United States of America by Vail-Ballou Press, Binghamton, New York.

Library of Congress Cataloging-in-Publication Data
Levy, Donald, 1936–
    Freud among the philosophers : the psychoanalytic unconscious and its
philosophical critics / Donald Levy.
        p.   cm.
    Includes bibliographical references and index.
    ISBN 0-300-06632-5 (cloth : alk. paper)
    1. Psychoanalysis and philosophy.   2. Psychoanalytic
interpretation.   I. Freud, Sigmund, 1856–1939.   II. Title.
BF175.P45L48   1996
150.19'52 — dc20   96-2169
                                                                          CIP

A catalogue record for this book is available from the British Library.

The paper in this book meets the guidelines for permanence and durability of the Committee on Production Guidelines for Book Longevity of the Council on Library Resources.

10   9   8   7   6   5   4   3   2   1

In memory of my parents and of my sister

Contents

. . . .

Acknowledgments

This book had its origins in work I did for the doctoral degree in philosophy at Cornell University. Richard Boyd advised me during the process of writing my thesis, and I am grateful for his efforts on my behalf. Paul Edwards and Marilyn Hamilton provided invaluable suggestions and support during the years in which I struggled to turn some of the ideas in my thesis into articles (Levy, 1983a, 1983b, 1987, 1988). The long incubation that transformed those articles into this book could not have succeeded without the intervention of many people, prominent among them being my colleagues at Brooklyn College and Michael Eigen, whose numerous hints and riddling remarks helped greatly. Several sabbatical leaves made possible by the administration at Brooklyn College provided me with the time I needed to write. I am indebted to Adolph Grünbaum for corresponding with me concerning my review (1988) of his book. Marcia Cavell and Paul Robinson encouraged my work at a crucial time, as did David Richards; from start to finish, his advice, assistance, encouragement, and support sustained me while I wrote this book, as did the kindness and enthusiasm of Diane Richards.

. . . .

Introduction

For as long as psychoanalysis has existed, its central concept, that of unconscious mental activity, has been the object of hostile scrutiny by philosophers. Is the idea of unconscious mental activity the intellectual revolution it claims to be or merely pseudo-science, myth-making, ideology? The influence of psychoanalysis in our culture has become so pervasive that the answer to these philosophical questions cannot help but affect the many uses other disciplines have found for psychoanalysis. So philosophical inquiry into the legitimacy of psychoanalytic concepts bears directly upon other disciplines in ways few other contemporary philosophical inquiries do.

It is fascinating to speculate about why psychoanalysis has been so influential for the better part of this century, although the question is beyond the scope of this book. What does psychoanalysis offer that explains its pervasiveness? Of course, ideas drawn from psychoanalytic inquiry have also come to play the role of something like a common language, understood or employed by many who have no contact with psychoanalysts or their writings. How can a case history from the early decades of this century arouse the interest of an audience much wider than the relatively small group of those professionally concerned? Perhaps the answer can be found in something we have come to value greatly in the modern world—something psychoanalysis offers in abundance—namely, the opportunity to participate, directly or vicariously, in the unfolding of individual subjectivity; perhaps it is because psychoanalysis inquires into the self without imposed assumptions, or with as few as possible, that it has played this role. The idea that if all assumptions or conventions are suspended, then what is natural or real must reveal itself can itself be seen as a convention of modern thought; it is noteworthy that none of the critics examined in this book rejects the possibility that this might occur, although all doubt whether psychoanalysis succeeds in it. Probably, it is Wittgenstein who most poignantly experienced the difficulties inherent in viewing the individual mind wholly apart from traditional assumptions about its nature. His criticism of psychoanalysis is in some ways the most complex, including, as it does, different points to which each of the other critics confine themselves.

For Wittgenstein, psychoanalysis essentially *imposes* interpretations, rather than unfolding them as it claims. According to Wittgenstein, a psychoanalytic interpretation essentially involves a myth-like (that is, predetermined) explanation, imposed on a mental state that reduces it to something familiar and common where, nevertheless, the assent of the person involved is the criterion of correctness. There is a fundamental tension here, for once the mental state has been identified, its correct explanation would seem to be given by the mythology applied, yet the assent or nonassent of the patient is supposed to be dispositive. It would be fair to say of Wittgenstein, I think, that for him, psychoanalysis is a kind of crude religion, one that does not even realize that that is what it is.

Wittgenstein's is the most powerful and persuasive statement of this criticism which, if valid, would undermine one of the main claims Freud's ideas have on our attention, in my view. Wittgenstein's criticism itself rests on a viewpoint closer to a religious than to a scientific approach; it is in this regard that it differs from the other criticisms examined in this book, where the alleged failure of psychoanalysis to conform to the scientific method is the main philosophical issue. Wittgenstein's comparison of psychoanalytic interpretation to myth-making rests on a crucial confusion, I argue, between the form of interpretive statements and the form of the dream or symptom that gave rise to those interpretations. Of course, Freud treats dreams and symptoms as having meaning, saying things; the condensations and displacements in dreams say, "This is really this," "This is all a repetition of that." By contrast, for Freud, the form of the interpretation is: "This dream *says* 'This is really this.' " Wittgenstein is able to make it plausible to treat interpretations as mythological in nature only by assuming that interpretations have the same logical form as the dreams and symptoms they describe. This confusion, I argue, underlies the fear, not at all peculiar to Wittgenstein, that psychoanalytic interpretations are essentially *reductive* in nature. I believe this is the essence of the religious objection to psychoanalytic interpretation, which can seem fundamentally subversive of religious interpretation of the same phenomena. For Wittgenstein, psychoanalysis tries too hard to be scientific and so destroys what is individual in us in the process of seeking to reduce mental phenomena to mere law-governed data. In this process, what is essential about the mind eludes the psychoanalyst's awareness, as well as the patient's. This reading of Wittgenstein on psychoanalysis has been missed by many who assume his criticisms are the same as those of the opposing scientific school, who object to Freud's ideas and those of his followers precisely because they are not scientific enough.[1] Much of the fascination of Wittgenstein's discussion of these issues is the indirect means he takes to address them; for he does not explicitly raise the question of the relation of psychoanalysis to religion but rather, I believe, alludes to it in ways that are always suggestive, surprising, and perhaps more illuminating than if he had addressed the question explicitly. A large body of valuable literature on religion's relation to psychoanalysis exists, much of it by psychoana-

---

1. Readers who wish to pursue what I have called the religious critique of psychoanalysis along lines similar to Wittgenstein's can hardly do better than to read K. Frieden's *Freud's Dream of Interpretation*.

lysts, since the authors are generally not at all critical of the psycho-analytic enterprise itself, in contrast to Wittgenstein. I have not dealt with it here.

If Wittgenstein objects to psychoanalysis because he thinks it reduces the meaning we can find within ourselves, the main criticism of Freud's central ideas aside from Wittgenstein has been that those ideas are not reductive enough; what is wanted is real scientific knowledge, which, despite Freud's promise, psychoanalysis does not succeed in producing. It is remarkable that this vast difference in viewpoint between Wittgenstein and the other philosophical critics of psychoanalysis, many of whom were influenced by him, has taken so long to be perceived, and not only in regard to psychoanalysis. As far as I know, the first chapter of this book provides the only comprehensive, critical overview of Wittgenstein's ideas on the subject of psychoanalysis.[2]

In chapter 2, after examining the argument based on posthypnotic suggestion, one of Freud's main proofs for the existence of unconscious mental activity, I then consider William James's criticism of all proofs of such phenomena. For James, the very idea of unconscious mental activity, is incoherent, that is, self-contradictory. I argue that James's reasons for holding this view are weaker than he realized. Besides, for James, unconscious mental activity is unnecessary because any phenomenon whose explanation appears to require the concept can in all cases be explained instead by other means, that is, by reference to conscious ideas that are quickly gone or are unattended to or, failing that, by reference to brain processes. Despite the elegance and sophistication of James's treatment and his apparently successful demolition of a great many persuasive arguments for the existence of unconscious mental activity, I argue that there are stresses in James's approach, stresses that come progressively to the fore in the mind of the careful reader, as James's critique progresses. I believe there are signs that he himself began to sense these prob-

---

2. J. Bouveresse's *Wittgenstein Reads Freud* appeared too late for discussion here. This work mainly defends Wittgenstein's views, with conclusions very different from mine.

lems, although he does not openly acknowledge them. This new way of reading James seems to me to deepen interest in his struggle with the idea of unconscious mental activity, an idea that, on a superficial reading, he can seem to have rather airily dismissed. What gives permanent interest to his (partially concealed) struggle against that idea is the extreme plausibility of his rejection of it; once one accepts his starting point, it is not at all easy to see how one can avoid agreeing with his rejection. I contrast James's treatment with Freud's favorite posthypnotic suggestion argument, an argument that I believe fails, although Freud never realized this. My conclusion that the argument fails, however, leaves the psychoanalytic concept of unconscious mental activity itself unscathed, in my view.

Freud's posthypnotic suggestion argument *in support of* unconscious mental activity fails, I argue, for reasons comparable to those that also undermine the validity of James's *criticism* of such arguments; both fail to take seriously what Freud himself elsewhere indicated was the central role that resistance plays in the attribution of unconscious mental activity in psychoanalysis.

Now the phenomenon of resistance is easily misunderstood; it is a mistake to assume that it consists in nothing more than the opposition that patients present to the interpretive efforts of psychoanalysts or others; thus, Freud writes:

> How are we to arrive at a knowledge of the unconscious? It is of course only as something conscious that we know it, after it has undergone transformation or translation into something conscious. Psycho-analytic work shows us every day that translation of this kind is possible. In order that this should come about, the person under analysis must overcome certain resistances—the same resistances as those which, earlier, made the material concerned into something repressed by rejecting it from the conscious.[3]

Clearly, what Freud means by resistance cannot be defined merely in terms of the patient's opposition to treatment—for that opposition is seen here as a manifestation of something intrapsychic that existed

3. Freud, "The Unconscious," 14:166.

prior to the attempted treatment. In each of the cases Freud mentions there — parapraxes (slips of all kinds), dreams, symptoms (and even jokes, which he mentions elsewhere) — our own mental state seems to us to mean something, while at the same time we do not know what it means. This paradoxical experience is at the core of psychoanalytic ascriptions of unconscious mental activity and is strikingly absent, both from Freud's own posthypnotic suggestion argument, as well as from the main cases James considers in seeking to show the avoidability of such ascriptions. (Resistance is perhaps to be found hovering, implicitly, in the very last of the arguments he considers, but he does not acknowledge it.) I argue that resistance to one's own ideas and wishes cannot be accounted for in any of the ten ways James considers; indeed, there are reasons why no explanations of the sorts he considers are likely to be adequate to explain the experience of resistance.

Chapter 3 deals with A. MacIntyre's argument that the unconscious in psychoanalysis is unobservable in a way that separates it from legitimate unobservables in science; unlike them, the psychoanalytic unconscious is dispensable in principle, he argues. By contrast, I show that various misunderstandings of what psychoanalysis means by the unconscious have led him to treat it as intrinsically unobservable. For psychoanalysis, either the unconscious is not absolutely unobservable, or else being unobservable is not a stigma unique to it; if it is unobservable, ordinary conscious ideas and wishes will have to classed as unobservable, too. MacIntyre does not consider the possibility that a technique like free association might make the unconscious not absolutely unobservable. I discuss the conceptions of unobservability and observability in contemporary philosophy of science, which seem to me to focus in an artificial way on the idea of an entity or property whose essence it is to be unobservable (or observable) — that is, on the idea of an entity or property that is unobservable (or observable) in all possible worlds, which, as I try to show, is absurd.

Chapter 4 examines A. Grünbaum's critique of psychoanalysis, which can best be seen as the polar opposite of Wittgenstein's on the central question (around which this entire book revolves): What is the criterion of a psychoanalytic interpretation's truth? For Grünbaum, the assent of the subject of the interpretation has no evidentiary status, whereas for Wittgenstein, such assent is the only criterion there is. So, for Grünbaum, psychoanalytic interpretations are untestable within the confines of the therapeutic situation; only extraclinical testing can determine their truth, and these tests, on the whole, have not been undertaken. In response to Grünbaum's criticisms, I show that his argument rests on a false dichotomy between intra- and extraclinical evidence, for which he has no criterion, and on attributing views to Freud about the testing of his hypotheses that cannot really be derived from his writings. Thus, Grünbaum attributes to Freud the claim that the only evidence for the truth of a psychoanalytic interpretation is its success in removing or reducing pathology, whereas Freud actually offered a wide variety of different kinds of evidence that he took to be supportive apart from, and even in the absence of, therapeutic success. Besides, I argue that Grünbaum himself is committed to the view that he attributes to Freud — namely, that therapeutic success is the empirical basis on which Freud's theories stand or fall. (In the appendix, I examine how it is possible for Grünbaum to be committed to this view without necessarily realizing that he is.) In practical terms, without a well-defined distinction between intra- and extraclinical evidence, Grünbaum's repudiation of intraclinical testing leads to three sorts of difficulties in the extraclinical testing of psychoanalytic hypotheses he proposes; first, I argue that when detached from their clinical setting, the hypotheses cease to be genuinely psychoanalytic ones. Then, if those hypotheses are testable extraclinically at all, it is by relying implicitly on intraclinical methods and data. Absent that reliance, the hypotheses cease being really testable at all, since their key terms, *unconscious ideas* and *unconscious wishes,* when detached from resistance and transference phenomena typical of clinical inquiry, lose their meaning. Indicating the ways in which these difficulties arise in the main task of chapter 4.

The chapters of this book comprise the main pillars supporting what I think of as the argument of psychoanalysis: that is, they attempt to deal rationally with philosophical objections to psychoanalysis from very different opposing viewpoints.[4] Each chapter deals with a criticism that seems to me to have some persuasive power and that is also widely held. In each case, I have focused on the formulation of this criticism as it occurs in the thought of that philosophical critic who, in my opinion, has formulated it most memorably. I believe that the critics I examine share basic misunderstandings — not at all obvious ones — of a few psychoanalytic ideas and that when these are cleared up, their criticisms are neutralized. Of course, that is very far from providing a positive justification for the numerous things Freud, and psychoanalysts after him, have claimed. But there is a limit to what can be expected from philosophical inquiry in a field such as this.

Nevertheless, in addition to undoing the confusions and misunderstandings that stand in the way of our seeing psychoanalysis as it is, it is also possible to show that we have gained something important from it, something new and original, not available elsewhere in modern thought, or in previous inquiries of whatever sort into the human mind. The project of "unfolding" individual subjectivity is one that psychoanalysis can claim to have advanced in a specific way, as I argue in the afterword.

4. A valuable response to Freud's (mainly) nonphilosophical critics can be found in Paul Robinson's *Freud and His Critics,* which also contains a chapter on Grünbaum.

1

. . . .

Wittgenstein's Critique
of Psychoanalysis

Wittgenstein's thoughts on psychoanalysis are mainly found in five places in material so far published: "Wittgenstein's Lectures in 1930–33," as reported by G. E. Moore;[1] the *Blue Book* (dictated 1933–34); "Lectures on Aesthetics" (1938) and "Conversations on Freud" (dating from the same period as Part I of *Philosophical Investigations*), both preserved in Rush Rhees's notes in *Lectures and Conversations*; and notes written by Wittgenstein collected under the title *Culture and Value*, edited by G. H. von Wright and translated by Peter Winch.[2] The total number of pages in these works actually devoted to psychoanalysis is small, but what is recorded there is of interest for several reasons. Much of what philosophers and psychoanalysts are writing today, both in defense of and in an attack upon psychoanalysis, repeats and varies ideas earlier expressed clearly and

1. Supplemented by remarks recorded by Alice Ambrose and Margaret MacDonald in *Wittgenstein's Lectures*, 39–40.

2. Moore, "Wittgenstein's Lectures in 1930–33"; Wittgenstein, *Blue and Brown Books*; Wittgenstein, *Lectures and Conversations*; Wittgenstein, *Culture and Value*.

forcefully by Wittgenstein. I believe that there are inconsistencies among these different passages from Wittgenstein and that his view of psychoanalysis is mistaken; but there is a progression in his thoughts that I have tried to retrace and criticize and that I think suggests several important points about psychoanalytic interpretation.

According to Wittgenstein, psychoanalysis is not a science; rather, it is a mythology. Since the sole criterion of a psychoanalytic interpretation's correctness is the subject's assent,[3] such an interpretation is not a discovery, it is not predictive, nor is establishing its correctness a matter of evidence.[4] That psychoanalysis is a mythology results first from its being a kind of persuasion, that is, something we believe as a result of someone imposing their views upon us, so that if they had imposed something different upon us, we would believe something different. Further, interpretations are "only a 'wonderful representation,'" a sort of mythology, since they are of the form "This is really only this," "This is *really* this," "This is all a repetition of something that has happened before."[5]

ASSENT AS CRITERION

Wittgenstein emphasized that psychoanalytic interpretations — in terms of unconscious thoughts, feelings, wishes — are different from explanations in the physical sciences: "He asserted that a psychoanalysis is successful only if the patient agrees to the explanation offered by the analyst. He said there is nothing analogous to this in Physics; and that what a patient agrees to can't be a *hypothesis* as to the cause of his laughter [the example in the portion preceding the excerpt], but only that so-and-so was the *reason* why he laughed. He explained that the patient who agrees did not think of this reason at the moment when he laughed, and that to say that he thought of it

---

3. Moore, "Wittgenstein's Lectures in 1930–33," 310; Wittgenstein, *Lectures and Conversations,* 18.

4. Wittgenstein, *Lectures and Conversations,* 18, 25, 27, 42.

5. Moore, "Wittgenstein's Lectures in 1930–33," 309; Wittgenstein, *Lectures and Conversations,* 24–25, 27, 43, 51–52.

'subconsciously' 'tells you nothing as to what was happening at the moment when he laughed.' "[6]

Wittgenstein does not here deny the sense of saying that someone was thinking something subconsciously; he wishes only to combat the attempt to model such a claim on statements describing what a person was thinking at a certain point in time. The patient's agreement is necessary in order for us to know that an interpretation is correct; Wittgenstein seems to mean that it is the only way we can know this. I believe that is the force of the following passage as well:

> Sometimes he [Freud] says that the right solution, or the right analysis, is the one which satisfies the patient. Sometimes he says that the doctor knows what the right solution or analysis of the dream is whereas the patient doesn't: the doctor can say that the patient is wrong.
>
> The reason why he calls one sort of analysis the right one, does not seem to be a matter of evidence.[7]

Since the doctor can have no evidence as his reason for judging a solution to be the right one apart from the satisfaction of the patient, Wittgenstein seems to be expressing skepticism here that the doctor (that is, the analyst) can ever know what the right solution or analysis of a dream is when the patient is not satisfied, or prior to the patient's indication of satisfaction.

So I shall summarize Wittgenstein's view by saying that assent or agreement by the patient is the criterion of an interpretation's correctness. Wittgenstein appears to have connected this to another important idea — that an interpretation is "only a 'wonderful representation,' " "not a matter of discovery, but of persuasion," a "mythology that is offered or imposed on one . . . a powerful mythology."[8] This connection is clear in Wittgenstein's remarks in "Conversations on Freud":

> Freud in his analysis provides explanations which many people are inclined to accept. He emphasizes that people are *dis*-inclined to accept

6. Moore, "Wittgenstein's Lectures in 1930–33," 310.

7. Wittgenstein, *Lectures and Conversations*, 42.

8. Moore, "Wittgenstein's Lectures in 1930–33," 309; Wittgenstein, *Lectures and Conversations*, 27, 52.

them. But if the explanation is one which people are disinclined to accept, it is highly probable that it is also one which they are *inclined* to accept. And this is what Freud has actually brought out. Take Freud's view that anxiety is always a repetition in some way of the anxiety we felt at birth. He does not establish this by reference to evidence — for he could not do so. But it is an idea that has marked attraction. It has the attraction which mythological explanations have, explanations which say that this is all a repetition of something that has happened before. And when people do accept or adopt this, then certain things seem much clearer and easier for them. So it is with the notion of the unconscious also.[9]

If there were something that could establish an interpretation's correctness other than the patient's agreeing to it, Wittgenstein could not treat the interpretation as mythology without further argument.

Wittgenstein sees the assent given to interpretations as attributable to something other than their truth; discussing Freud's notion of an *Urszene* Wittgenstein says: "Many people have, at some period, serious trouble in their lives — so serious as to lead to thoughts of suicide. This is likely to appear to one as something nasty, as a situation which is too foul to be a subject of tragedy. And it may then be an immense relief if it can be shown that one's life has the pattern rather of a tragedy — the tragic working out and repetition of a pattern which was determined by the primal scene."[10] From any point of view, it is hard to see what the patient is assenting to in accepting an interpretation; but if there were some way of showing interpretations to be true, independent of the subject's agreeing to them, speculation about what motivates people to accept them would be idle; presumably, people's reasons for accepting interpretations would then be, or could be, based on the same evidence the analyst has, or could have, for making the interpretations in the first place. Assent as the criterion may not seem enough to warrant inferring that interpretations are mythological; after all, isn't assent the criterion for the truth of our descriptions of another person's thoughts, feelings,

9. Wittgenstein, *Lectures and Conversations*, 43. The point here concerns a very general claim — but Wittgenstein seems to mean it to apply to individual interpretations of the symptoms of particular people as well.

10. Ibid., 51.

wishes? But whereas the latter are or could be present in the subject's mind at a certain time, Wittgenstein has already indicated that attributions of unconscious mental states tell us nothing of what was going on in the mind of the person supposed to be acting out of unconscious thoughts, feelings, wishes.[11] More precisely, Wittgenstein says that such attributions tell us nothing of what was going on mentally while the person was acting out unconscious thoughts, and so on. For Wittgenstein, unconscious thoughts cannot be located in time the way conscious ones may be. So interpretations differ in important ways from other sorts of statements whose criterion is assent. The assent criterion and the absence of temporal location seem to lead naturally to the view that interpretations are mythological; perhaps this is why the assent criterion has been resisted by some supporters of psychoanalysis (for example, B. A. Farrell, J. O. Wisdom). An exception appears to be Freud himself; in "Constructions in Analysis"[12] and earlier in lecture three of *Introductory Lectures on Psychoanalysis*,[13] versions of the assent criterion are offered.

"UNCONSCIOUS TOOTHACHE"

But there is another strand to Wittgenstein's views on psychoanalysis, in addition to his emphasis on assent as the criterion, that has found a place in subsequent discussion. It occurs in the *Blue Book* but first appeared in the 1930–33 *Lectures.*

> He said that Freud had really discovered phenomena and connections not previously known, but that he talked as if he had found out that there were in the human mind "unconscious" hatreds, volitions, etc., and that this was very misleading, because we think of the differences between a "conscious" and an "unconscious" hatred as like that between a "seen" and an "unseen" chair. He said that, in fact, the grammar of "felt" and "unfelt" hatred is quite different from that of "seen" and "unseen" chair,

---

11. Moore, "Wittgenstein's Lectures in 1930–33," 310.
12. Freud, "Constructions in Analysis," 23:261–63 .
13. Freud, *Introductory Lectures on Psycho-Analysis.*

just as the grammar of "artificial" flower is quite different from that of "blue" flower. He suggested that "unconscious toothache," if "unconscious" were used as Freud used it, might be necessarily bound up with a physical body, whereas "conscious toothache" is not so bound up.[14]

The "phenomena and connections not previously known" appear to be behavioral phenomena — hence the antithesis with what is in the human mind. This is clearer in a related passage: "(Should we say that there are cases when a man despises another man and doesn't know it; or should we describe such cases by saying that he doesn't despise him but unintentionally behaves toward him in a way — speaks to him in a tone of voice, etc. — which in general would go together with despising him? Either form of expression is correct; but they may betray different tendencies of the mind.)"[15] The clearest statement of this other line of thought occurs earlier in the *Blue Book*. There, Wittgenstein is trying to illustrate one of his major themes, that phenomena do not impose on us a single correct form of description. There is, for example, no single correct answer to the question, "When I feel fear, but don't have any object in mind, must there be some object I'm unaware of, or can fear exist without an object?"

> To understand this, examine the following example: — It might be found practical to call a certain state of decay in a tooth, not accompanied by what we commonly call toothache, "unconscious toothache," and to use in such a case the expression that we have toothache, but don't know it. It is in just this sense that psychoanalysis talks of unconscious thoughts, acts of volition, etc. Now is it wrong in this sense to say that I have a toothache but don't know it? There is nothing wrong about it, as it is just a new terminology and can at any time be retranslated into ordinary language.[16]

The point of this passage (and of others like it) seems to conflict with Wittgenstein's emphasis on assent as the criterion for the presence of unconscious mental states. If unconscious contempt, for example, can be attributed to a person on the basis of contemptuous behavior

14. Moore, "Wittgenstein's Lectures in 1930–33," 304.
15. Wittgenstein, *Blue Book*, 30.
16. Ibid., 22–23.

alone, how can assent be the criterion of such an interpretation's correctness? For in deciding whether a subject's behavior is of a contemptuous sort, the assent of the subject is, of course, not needed, just as assent is unnecessary in deciding whether someone has "unconscious toothache." The state of one's teeth settles that decisively. Another way in which this passage seems to conflict with the assertion that assent is the sole criterion is this: a person has an unconscious toothache for as long as the state of decay in the tooth is unaccompanied by pain in the tooth. So unconscious toothache has temporal duration; but Wittgenstein had earlier implied that unconscious mental processes (for example, the reason for laughing at a joke) cannot be located in time. I believe the force of this model for unconscious mental processes is to conflate unconscious motivation with mere inadvertence or lack of awareness.

The *Blue Book* passage quoted above makes it clearer why Wittgenstein held it misleading to speak of unconscious mental processes at all;[17] unlike conscious ones, unconscious mental processes signify nothing more than bodily conditions. So the price we pay for getting a criterion of correctness for interpretations other than assent is having to treat interpretations as mere redescriptions of behavior that tell us nothing about the mind. Wittgenstein presents us with this dilemma: if we treat assent as the criterion of interpretations, we are led to see interpretations as mythological; but if we treat them as confirmable in behavior, apart from assent, they then convey no new knowledge but merely redescribe behavior in a new, gratuitous terminology.

From a psychoanalytic point of view, the unconscious toothache model is unsatisfactory; there is no condensation or displacement of ideas observable in it, no primary process thinking of the sort to be found in dreams and neurosis, and nothing in it to correspond to the phenomenon of resistance — that is, to the "special hindrance" that "evidently deflects our investigations from our own self and prevents our obtaining a true knowledge of it."[18] Without a dental examina-

17. Moore, "Wittgenstein's Lectures in 1930–33," 304.
18. Freud, "The Unconscious," 14:170.

tion, who would expect to know whether they had an unconscious toothache? Yet people regularly act as if they would know if they were reacting to some unconscious idea. They vigorously and sincerely deny the influence of an unconscious motivation, in a way no one would deny an attribution of inadvertent behavior; and then, without any empirical inquiry comparable to a dental examination — that is, merely by being reminded of already known facts, they come to accept what they formerly denied. In considering a view similar to Wittgenstein's, Freud comments: "This attempt to equate what is unnoticed with what is unconscious is obviously made without taking into account the dynamic conditions involved, which were the decisive factors in forming the psycho-analytic view. . . . For it ignores [the fact that] the thought which was previously unnoticed is not recognized by consciousness, but often seems entirely alien and opposed to it and is promptly disavowed by it."[19] Earlier in the same work Freud remarks:

> We assert that the force which instituted the repression and maintains it is perceived as *resistance* during the work of analysis.
>
> Thus we obtain our concept of the unconscious from the theory of repression. The repressed is the prototype of the unconscious for us.[20]

Freud here contrasts his own idea of the unconscious, derived from "the work of analysis," with nonpsychoanalytic notions. So the unconscious toothache case is inadequate, and Freud's talk of unconscious thoughts cannot be "retranslated into ordinary language" in the way Wittgenstein's unconscious toothache model implies.

For Wittgenstein, assent by the patient is *the* criterion of an interpretation's correctness. If assent is achieved, the interpretation's correctness is established; if the interpretation is rejected, its falsity is proved. In the absence of acceptance it is impossible to know whether an interpretation is correct; without rejection, we cannot tell if one is false. If assent were decisive in this way, there could not be another criterion on a par with it; for, if there were, a conflict

19. Freud, *The Ego and the Id*, 19:16, n. 1.
20. Ibid., 14–15.

between such criteria would be possible, and then at least one would be not as decisive as supposed. The inference to be drawn from this is not necessarily that interpretations are mythological in nature; rather, something seems wrong with the general account of criteria presupposed here. We should not assume there is one thing that determines an interpretation's (or any statement's) correctness. By speaking in this way, Wittgenstein is arguing in sharp contrast to the dominant position he adopts in the *Philosophical Investigations,* where he emphasizes the multiplicity of criteria for statements. Wittgenstein had argued forcefully against the idea that there is always one absolutely right way to describe some given phenomenon — a form of representation identical with the form of the phenomenon. But his criticism of Freud seems to assume that there is one absolutely right way to verify the description of a phenomenon.[21] Rather, we should say that although assent will often be a criterion of correctness, other criteria are possible; there is no such thing as *the* criterion of correctness.

Much of what Freud says in "Constructions in Analysis" (1937) agrees with Wittgenstein's extreme emphasis on assent: the patient may deny that the interpretation is right at first but must finally assent, or else the interpretation is not correct or is incomplete. The assent must be of a special sort — that is, accompanied by, or leading to, associations — memories that "fit" the interpretation. Freud differs from Wittgenstein, however, when he speaks of many indirect forms of confirmation, "in every respect trustworthy," that an interpretation is correct. So sometimes the analyst knows what the right analysis is on the basis of the evidence, and sometimes confirmation must wait upon the patient's satisfaction; there is no need for a single, general answer to the question, "How do you know an interpretation is correct?"

This is contrary, I believe, to Wittgenstein's point. It may be that the criteria for an interpretation's correctness other than assent are nevertheless *assent-linked* — that is, they may be based on the patient's agreement with other statements, perhaps other interpreta-

21. Wittgenstein, *Lectures and Conversations,* 42.

tions, that entail or support the correctness of the unassented to interpretation. Or we may have evidence for believing the patient *would* assent to a statement whose truth is a criterion for the correctness of the interpretation. In these cases, the patient's assent is needed — but not to the individual interpretation. These possibilities are all contrary to Wittgenstein's meaning.[22] They all undermine the mythology charge, which I have suggested is based in part on the assumption that the sole criterion of an interpretation's correctness is the patient's assent to the particular interpretation.

It is tempting to think that Wittgenstein could hold that *the* criterion of correctness is the patient's assent while also contending that we may believe an interpretation is probably correct on the basis of other evidence — the passage from Moore by itself doesn't seem to contradict this.[23] I believe that "other evidence" is possible consistent with Wittgenstein's view — but only in a sense so restricted as to be immaterial to the mythology claim. For the only "other evidence" that Wittgenstein's view would admit, I think, would be evidence that assent can or will be achieved. The following quotations bring out how extreme Wittgenstein's position is on this point and also show the implication it has for him:

> You have to give the explanation that is accepted. This is the whole point of the explanation....
>
> 33. If you are led by psychoanalysis to say that really your motive was so and so, this is not a matter of discovery, but of persuasion. In a different way you could have been persuaded of something different. One thinks of certain results of psychoanalysis as a discovery Freud made as apart from something persuaded to you by a psychoanalyst, and I wish to say this is not the case.[24]

Wittgenstein's remark that no contrast is to be made between a "discovery" of psychoanalysis and "something persuaded to you by a psychoanalyst" lends support to the view that he can allow other evidence for an interpretation (other than assent) only if that evi-

22. E.g., ibid., and Moore, "Wittgenstein's Lectures in 1930–33," 310.
23. Moore, "Wittgenstein's Lectures in 1930–33," 310.
24. Wittgenstein, *Lectures and Conversations*, 18, 27.

dence is evidence that assent can or will be achieved. I think it follows that even if we allow other evidence to support an interpretation, if we do it in a way compatible with Wittgenstein's view, his claim that interpretations are no more than persuasions prevents that other evidence from being anything more than evidence concerning what the patient will, or can be persuaded to, assent to.

KINDS OF PSYCHOANALYTIC INTERPRETATIONS

Is Wittgenstein right to treat assent as the criterion? There are two issues here. One is the more factual question concerning the *kinds* of interpretations and the criteria employed by analysts. The other concerns why Wittgenstein determines the status of interpretations, given their criteria, in the strict way that he does.

On the first issue, it is a mistake to speak of interpretations in general — there are different sorts of interpretations that form parts of a construction in Freud's sense. Interpretations of unconscious content state the meanings of dreams and symptoms. But there are also interpretations of defenses or resistances to such meanings — for example, when they occur in free association, or when interpretations of content are made by the analyst. Defenses are unconscious procedures for warding off one's own psychic states, which are experienced as attacks on one's self-esteem — for example, projection, isolation, repression. They are manifested, when the patient does not simply deny or accept an interpretation but responds to it as to a threat and continues to avoid considering it. In contrast with symptoms, defenses often manifest themselves in behavior and feelings that seem right to the patient, are part of one's character. Interpretations of defenses are often verifiable apart from assent or prior to it; they relate to the patient's present life and can be identified without reference to the remote past. It seems pompous to defend the "verifiability" of such defense or resistance interpretations because often what is involved is so closely akin to what any sensitive human being with common sense does in judging the sincerity of others (and oneself). Interpretations of defenses differ insofar as they occur in a restricted context of extreme prolonged intimacy during which symptoms are openly discussed and in the course of prolonged free association. But to deny that such interpretations are ever known to be true apart from the assent of the patient would be like denying that we are ever justified in believing others to be insincere or rationalizing unless and until they agreed they were. Ordinarily aware nonpsychoanalysts do not think this way, and psychoanalysts ought not to, either.

In addition to the two sorts of interpretations so far distinguished, interpretations of formal elements in the patient's behavior are also possible — for example, changing facial expressions, ways of lying on the couch, ways of starting and finishing the session. "These formal elements of behaviour are part and parcel of the patient's *transference,* expressing both his general — lasting — sentiments towards the world, and his present — passing — attitudes towards a particular object — his analyst; consequently they have to be regarded as phenomena of some kind of *object-relation* — often of a primitive type — which has been revived in (or perhaps by) the psycho-analytical situation."[25] Balint clearly means to use the same behaviors as evidence, not only of the patient's present (unconscious) attitudes toward the analyst and of his general, lasting sentiments toward the world, but also as evidence of the object-relation that has been revived by the situation out of the past. When interpreted as evidence of past object-relations, the behaviors support interpretations that are more like interpretations of unconscious content in that assent is the main criterion. Whereas, when he interprets the same behavior as evidence of present unconscious attitudes, or as evidence of his general, lasting sentiments, these interpretations are more like resistance interpretations in that verification independent, in varying degrees, of assent is then possible. Roughly, resistance interpretations are like Wittgenstein's judgment of "unconscious toothache," whereas interpretations of content conform to what he says about interpreting a joke, where assent is needed. But neither of these models adequately covers all interpretations. If I am right to treat resistances as similar to Wittgenstein's "unconscious toothache," then it seems plausible to

25. Balint, *Primary Love and Psycho-analytic Technique,* 212.

treat the unconscious mental mechanisms in them (for example, projection) as locatable in time, as I already noted "unconscious toothache" to be. People do speak easily of those attacking another as projecting their own unacceptable feelings onto the other; they are unconsciously projecting *when* they attack the other. So even if the unconscious meaning of a joke cannot be placed in time, some unconscious mental processes can be — for example, the activation of defense mechanisms.

I have so far argued that assent is not the sole criterion for all interpretations; but even for those interpretations where assent may be the sole criterion, Wittgenstein is mistaken to suppose that there is no contrast to be made between what is discovered and what is persuaded. There is no initial presumption in favor of Wittgenstein's view; there is no reason to suppose that whenever a proposition may have assent as its sole criterion then no difference can be drawn between persuasion and discovery of its truth. In trying to remind someone what they were going to say but forgot, assent on their part is the criterion that we have gotten it right, but there is not even the temptation to confuse their accepting our suggestion because it is right with their accepting it because we have persuaded them. Wittgenstein gives the following related example:

> 37. "What is in my mind when I say so and so?"* I write a sentence. One word isn't the one I need. I find the right word. "What is it I want to say? Oh yes, that is what I wanted." The answer in these cases is the one that satisfied you, e.g., someone says (as we often say in philosophy): "I will tell you what is at the back of your mind: . . . "
> "Oh yes, quite so."
> The criterion for its being the one that was in your mind is that when I tell you, you agree.
>
> *Compare: 'What people really want to say is so and so' — R.[26]

When the reply is "Oh yes, quite so," was the person persuaded of something or did they realize or discover something? Persuasion does not seem likely because it seems implausible to say that with a

26. Wittgenstein, *Lectures and Conversations*, 18.

different argument, they could have been persuaded of another result, which Wittgenstein seems to regard as characteristic of persuasions.[27] Besides, other evidence might be available to document what was at the back of a person's mind — that is, evidence other than indications of what they can or will be persuaded to accept. There might be evidence, both of what is at the back of their mind, as well as of their inability or unwillingness to be persuaded to assent to it. Written notes would be an example of the first; the person's well-known disagreeableness of the second.

It seems doubtful that Wittgenstein would be willing to say that nothing was discovered in the examples quoted above — that these were instances of persuasion. If this is right, we must ask how psychoanalytic interpretations differ from the philosopher's telling us what is in the back of our minds. Of both he claims assent is the criterion; why, then, is the former a matter of persuasion, the latter not? The following remark needs to be considered, because it seems to imply that the latter (the philosopher's telling us what is in the back of our minds) *is* a matter of persuasion:

> 35. I very often draw your attention to certain differences, e.g., in these classes I try to show you that Infinity is not so mysterious as it looks. What I'm doing is also persuasion. If someone says: "There is not a difference," and I say: "There is a difference," I am persuading, I am saying, "I don't want you to look at it like that."* Suppose I wished to show you how very misleading the expressions of Cantor are. You ask: "What do you mean, it is misleading? Where does it lead you to?"
>
> *I am saying I want you to look at the thing in a different way. — T.[28]

Wittgenstein sees his philosophy as persuasion; the "also" in the second sentence means "like Freud" (see Remark 34, which is presented below). But here it is persuasion that something (for example, infinity) ought to be looked at one way rather than another. The persuasion is achieved by pointing out differences in the thing that were not seen or not considered important. This philosophical per-

27. Ibid., 27.
28. Ibid.

suasion is different from "saying what is in the back of someone's mind" because assent is the criterion of the latter, but presumably not of how to think about infinity. There seems to be some ambiguity in Wittgenstein's mind over whether philosophical discussion involves discovery or persuasion; he once remarked that he did not believe that G. E. Moore would *recognize* a *correct* solution in philosophy if he were presented with one.[29] That there can be such a thing as a correct solution in philosophy seems at odds with the idea that philosophical arguments are cases of persuasion, if he also regards it as characteristic of persuasion that "in a different way you could have been persuaded of something different."[30]

ARE PSYCHOANALYTIC INTERPRETATIONS MYTHOLOGIES?

Whatever is supposed to be wrong with psychoanalytic interpretations, according to Wittgenstein, it cannot merely be that they have assent as the criterion, since saying what is at the back of someone's mind shares that feature. Nor can it be that interpretations are mere instances of persuasion, since he thought the same is true of the right way to think about Infinity. To see what is objectionable in psychoanalytic interpretation for Wittgenstein, we need to explore his conception of a mythology. The claim that attributions of unconscious mental activity comprise a mythology is an idea Wittgenstein might have found in William James, but Wittgenstein goes on to say more about it.[31] That psychoanalytic interpretations are mythological in character depends,[32] for him, on the prior view that an interpretation is "'only a 'wonderful representation'"[33] of

29. Malcolm, *Ludwig Wittgenstein,* 66.

30. Wittgenstein, *Lectures and Conversations,* 27. If Wittgenstein meant that there is nothing more to (philosophical) correctness than persuasiveness, and that is what Moore could not recognize, the view seems paradoxical, since the claim that the correct solution in philosophy is *not* a persuasion must also be a persuasion, and so must be correct. So Moore's inability to recognize what is correct was correct, after all.

31. James, *Principles of Psychology,* 169–70.

32. Wittgenstein, *Lectures and Conversations,* 50–51.

33. Moore, "Wittgenstein's Lectures in 1930–33," 309.

the form "This is really only this,"[34] "This is *really* this,"[35] "This is all a repetition of something that has happened before."[36]

> 34. Those sentences have the form of persuasion in particular which say "This is *really* this." [This means — R] there are certain differences which you have been persuaded to neglect.* It reminds me of that marvellous motto: "Everything is what it is and not another thing. The dream is not bawdy, it is something else."

> *This means you are neglecting certain things and have been persuaded to neglect them. — R.[37]

Whether the repetition is of something that has happened before to other people or to the patient alone, the interpretation persuades the patient, imposes upon him to ignore the differences between his own present case and the others. For Wittgenstein, psychoanalytic interpretations ignore differences; philosophical persuasions (of which this argument is itself an instance) bring out differences.[38] In short, it is not merely because interpretations are unverifiable apart from assent that they are mythological in a defective sense. The real trouble, which gives point to these verification problems, for Wittgenstein, is that interpretations persuade people to ignore differences between their own present case and the general pattern in the proposed interpretation. Something of this is suggested in a remark his friend M. O. Drury remembers, "I was telling him of some psychiatric symptoms that puzzled me greatly. Wittgenstein said: 'You should never cease to be amazed at symptoms mental patients show. If I became mad the thing I would fear most would be your commonsense attitude. That you would take it all as a matter of course that I should be suffering from delusions.' "[39] This new point comes out

34. Wittgenstein, *Lectures and Conversations*, 24.
35. Ibid., 27.
36. Ibid., 43.
37. Ibid., 27. The dream referred to will be discussed below.
38. Ibid.
39. Drury, Symposium contribution in *Ludwig Wittgenstein*, 67.

more clearly when Wittgenstein examines Freud's interpretation of a particular dream, one its dreamer called beautiful.

Freud does something which seems to me immensely wrong. He gives what he calls an interpretation of dreams. In his book *The Interpretation of Dreams* he describes one dream which he calls a "beautiful dream" ["Ein schöner Traum" — R.].* A patient, after saying that she had had a beautiful dream, described a dream in which she descended from a height, saw flowers and shrubs, broke off the branch of a tree, etc. Freud shows what he calls the "meaning" of the dream. The coarsest sexual stuff, bawdy of the worst kind — if you wish to call it that — bawdy from A to Z. We know what we mean by bawdy. A remark sounds to the uninitiated harmless, but the initiated, say, chuckle when they hear it. Freud says the dream is bawdy. *Is* it bawdy? He shows relations between the dream images and certain objects of a sexual nature. The relation he establishes is roughly this. By a chain of circumstances, this leads to that, etc.† Does this prove that the dream is what is called bawdy? Obviously not. If a person talks bawdy, he doesn't say something which seems to him harmless, and is then psychoanalyzed.‡ Freud calls this dream "beautiful," putting "beautiful" in inverted commas. But wasn't the dream beautiful? I would say to the patient: "Do these associations make the dream not beautiful? It was beautiful.§ Why shouldn't it be?" I would say Freud had cheated the patient. Cf. scents made of things having intolerable smells. Could we therefore say: "The best scent is really all sulphuric acid?"‖ . . . Cf. "If we boil Redpath at 200 C. all that is left when the water vapour is gone is some ashes, etc.# This is all Redpath really is." Saying this might have a certain charm, but would be misleading, to say the least.

---

*Freud's "Ein schöner Traum" (*Die Traumdeutung,* Frankfurt: Fisher Bucherei, 1961, p. 240) does not contain the features of the "beautiful dream" described here. But the dream which does contain them (the "flowery dream" — "Blumentraum" — p. 289) is in fact described as "beautiful" or "pretty" ("schöne"): "Der schöne Traum wollte der Träumerin nach der Deutung gar nicht mehr gefallen." — Ed.

†From a flower to this, a tree to that, etc. — R.

‡You don't say a person talks bawdy when his intention is innocent. — T.

§This is what is called beautiful. — T.

‖If there is a connection between butyric acid which stinks and the best perfumes, could we on that account put "the best perfume" in quotes. — T.

#If we heat this man to 200 degrees Centigrade, the water evaporates . . ." — R.[40]

The analogies in the last sentences in the quote bring out how comparatively unimportant verification of interpretations is to Wittgenstein; for we can verify that a scent is made of sulphuric acid and of other foul-smelling things. We can verify what remains after a man's body has been boiled at 200 degrees C. It would still be wrong to say "This is all the fine-smelling scent really is — sulphuric acid and other foul-smelling things" or "This is all Redpath really is — vapour and ashes." Such claims are versions of the genetic fallacy in which a thing's nature is identified with the materials out of which it arose in the past, or to which it can be reduced in the future. Claims of this type are reductive in an eliminative way — they assert, for example, that fineness in scents (unlike foulness) and personality in humans (unlike corporeality) are illusory, and hence eliminable. So even if the symbolism in interpretations were verifiable, they would still be objectionable, for Wittgenstein, since they are of the form "This is *really* this," it seems — for example, "The 'beautiful' dream is really bawdy, it is not beautiful."

Wittgenstein's memory of the dream in question has led him seriously astray, however; here is the passage from Freud:

> The dreamer quite lost her liking for this pretty dream after it had been interpreted . . .
>
> (b) Main dream*: She was descending from a height over some strangely constructed palisades or fences, which were put together into large panels, and consisted of small squares of wattling. It was not intended for climbing over; she had trouble in finding a place to put her feet in and felt glad that her dress had not been caught anywhere, so that she had stayed respectable as she went along. She was holding a big branch in her hand; actually it was like a tree, covered over with red blossoms,

40. Wittgenstein, *Lectures and Conversations*, 23–24. Wittgenstein's claim that "We know what we mean by bawdy" is probably mistaken; the explanation given seems to confuse the meanings of bawdy and double entendre.

branching and spreading out. There was an idea of their being cherry-blossoms; but they also looked like double camellias, though of course those do not grow on trees. As she went down, first she had one, then suddenly two, and later again one. When she got down, the lower blossoms were already a good deal faded. Then she saw, after she got down, a manservant who—she felt inclined to say—was combing a similar tree, that is to say he was using a piece of wood to drag out some thick tufts of hair that were hanging down from it like moss. Some other workmen had cut down similar branches from a garden and thrown them into the road, where they lay about, so that a lot of people took some. But she asked whether that was all right—whether she might take one too. A young man (someone she knew, a stranger) was standing in the garden; she went up to ask how branches of that kind could be transplanted into her own garden. He embraced her; whereupon she struggled and asked him what he was thinking of and whether he thought people could embrace her like that. He said there was no harm in that; it was allowed. He then said he was willing to go into the other garden with her, to show her how the planting was done, and added something she could not understand. "Anyhow, I need three yards (later she gave it as: three square yards) or three fathoms of ground." It was as though he were asking her for something in return for his willingness, as though he intended to compensate himself in her garden, or as though he wanted to cheat some law or other, to get some advantage from it without causing her harm. Whether he really showed her something, she had no idea.

*Describing the course of her life.[41]

There is nothing in Freud's own words[42] that can be understood as "the dream is not beautiful; it is bawdy." Freud does not put the word *beautiful* in inverted commas. Whether the dream was or was not beautiful or bawdy is hardly the point for Freud; but the following quote shows him regarding the dream as representing both beautiful and bawdy trains of thought:

41. Freud *Interpretation of Dreams,* 5:347–48. All of Freud's footnotes that interpret specific features of the dream have been deleted, and his capitalization of those words to be given sexual interpretation has not been preserved. However, the words have not been altered.
42. Ibid.

And the same dream which expressed her joy at having succeeded in passing through life immaculately gave one glimpses at certain points (e.g., in the fading of the blossoms) of the contrary train of ideas — of her having been guilty of various sins against sexual purity (in her childhood, that is). In analysing the dream it was possible clearly to distinguish the two trains of thought, of which the consoling one seemed the more superficial and the self-reproachful one the deeper-lying — trains of thought which were diametrically opposed to each other but whose similar though contrary elements were represented by the same elements in the manifest dream.[43]

Freud calls the dream pretty, as Rush Rhees notes,[44] but says the patient stopped liking it after it was interpreted. Did she stop liking it because some of the elements in the dream were given sexual significance by Freud or were bawdy (that is, coarsely sexual) when interpreted? That is Wittgenstein's impression, as the last quoted passage from him shows; however, the patient had other good reasons to dislike the dream after it was interpreted, apart from the fact˙ that many apparently innocent elements in it were given sexual, or bawdy, meaning.

Wittgenstein appears to attribute to Freud the idea that the meaning of the dream is found simply by "decoding" the dream elements; since many of these stand for bawdy things, the dream is bawdy. If this were Freud's view, there might be some point in seeing the genetic fallacy in interpretations. Freud does say the dream elements are to be taken separately;[45] the apparent connection between them should be treated as an "unessential illusion," for the purposes of interpretation,[46] that is, in applying free association. But Freud emphasizes that it is the process of the dream-work that is essential in interpreting dreams.[47] The process by which the dream element arises from its meaning is as important as what the element stands for. Besides, "the dream-work is under some kind of necessity to

43. Ibid., 319.
44. Wittgenstein, *Lectures and Conversations*, 23n. 4.
45. Freud, *Interpretation of Dreams*, 4:104 and 449.
46. Ibid., 449.
47. Freud, *New Introductory Lectures on Psycho-Analysis*, 22:8.

combine all the sources which have acted as stimuli for the dream into a single unity in the dream itself."[48] The dream quoted above is taken from "The Dream-Work," chapter 4 of *The Interpretation of Dreams.* Freud means that dream's relation to the introductory dream to illustrate the way causality is represented in dreams. It is important to realize that we are not reading a case history in discussing Freud's interpretation of the main dream above or in the introductory dream that follows; so we do not know what use the dream found in therapy.

For Freud, the meaning of the main dream is alluded to in the footnote he attached to the main dream: the dream describes the course of her life. This dream derives its sense from the dream introducing it, which Freud regards as representing the causal conditions for the life represented in the main dream. Here is the introductory dream, with Freud's remarks:

> She went into the kitchen, where her two maids were, and found fault with them for not having got her "bite of food" ready. At the same time she saw a very large quantity of common kitchen crockery standing upside down in the kitchen drain; it was piled up in heaps. The two maids went to fetch some water and had to step into a kind of river which came right up to the house or into the yard. The main dream then followed. . . . The introductory dream related to the dreamer's parents' home. No doubt she had often heard her mother using the words that occurred in the dream. The heaps of common crockery were derived from a modest hardware shop which was located in the same building. The other part of the dream contained a reference to her father, who used always to run after the maids and who eventually contracted a fatal illness during a flood. (The house stood near a river-bank.) Thus the thought concealed behind the introductory dream ran as follows: "Because I was born in this house, in such mean and depressing circumstances . . ." The main dream took up the same thought and presented it in a form modified by wish-fulfillment: "I am of high descent." Thus the actual underlying thought was: "Because I am of such low descent, the course of my life has been so and so."[49]

48. Ibid., 179 and 488ff.
49. Freud, *Interpretation of Dreams*, 4:315.

Clearly, the patient had good reason to dislike the dream after it was interpreted, apart from the fact that many apparently innocent elements in it were given sexual, or bawdy, meaning.

Wittgenstein's recollection of the content of the main dream is importantly incomplete, "A patient . . . described a dream in which she descended from a height, saw flowers and shrubs, broke off the branch of a tree, etc."[50] Wittgenstein supposes the rest of the dream is pretty in much the same way as the part he mentions is pretty. But there is also the dreamer's struggle against the young man who tries to embrace her and who seems to want "to compensate himself in her garden . . . to cheat some law or other, to get some advantage from it without causing her harm."[51] Wittgenstein would be right to object if Freud had taken a wholly pretty dream or one entirely without sexual content and showed its sexual symbolism in such a way as to persuade that the dream was not really pretty. But the dream itself is sexually suggestive and does not have a pretty ending, even if its sexual suggestiveness is ignored. The dream is not pretty after Freud is through interpreting it in conjunction with the introductory dream; but then, the dream was not wholly pretty before Freud got to it.

According to Freud, the dreamer sees the mean and depressing aspects of her early home situation as the causes of her bad life. For Wittgenstein, in such cases "it may then be an immense relief if it can be shown that one's life has the pattern rather of a tragedy — the tragic working out and repetition of a pattern which was determined."[52]

WHAT IS THE FORM OF A
PSYCHOANALYTIC INTERPRETATION?

Wittgenstein supposes the purpose of an interpretation is to explain why the patient *is* fated to repeat — "This is all a repetition of

50. Wittgenstein, *Lectures and Conversations*, 23.
51. Freud, *Interpretation of Dreams*, 5:348.
52. Wittgenstein, *Lectures and Conversations*, 51.

something that has happened before" is the form of an interpretation for him. But this is false. The interpretation does bring out that the patient imagines that she is fated in this way, which may not have been obvious; and it explains why she imagines this. The immense relief Wittgenstein speaks of would be resistance to the interpretation, not a sign of insight or acceptance. "This is *really* this" or "This is all a repetition of something that has happened before" is not the form of an interpretation, as Wittgenstein supposes; it is the form of a symptom or dream in which "there is a striking tendency to *condensation,* an inclination to form fresh unities out of elements which in our waking thought we should certainly have kept separate . . . the existence of quite insignificant points in common between two elements is enough to allow the dream-work to replace one by the other in all further operations."[53] This point about the correct form of psychoanalytic interpretations suggests that Wittgenstein is mistaken in treating such interpretations as part of a mythology. It is the patient's dreams and symptoms that manifest a mythology that the interpretations are meant to explain. Interpretations are about the mythologies of patients.[54] A similar confusion probably underlies Karl Kraus's famous epigram: "Psychoanalysis is that mental disease whose therapy it claims to be."[55] The remark would be apt if psychoanalytic interpretations asserted that the condensations and displacements found in dreams and symptoms were true of the world outside the patient's mind — that is, if interpretations were of the form "This is really this."

Wittgenstein's account of the "beautiful dream" illustrates how he has misunderstood the whole business of interpreting — the form of an interpretation. He criticizes psychoanalytic interpretations because he thinks they are crudely reductive, that is, eliminative; how-

53. Freud, *Outline of Psycho-Analysis,* 23:167–68.

54. It is possible to distinguish myth from mythology, so that the latter signifies a branch of knowledge studying myths. But *mythology* can also mean a body of myths, and this is certainly what Wittgenstein means to say is the category in which psychoanalysis should be included (*Lectures and Conversations,* 51–52).

55. Kraus, *Werke,* 3:351.

ever, if interpretations are not of the form "This is *really* this," in Wittgenstein's sense, then Wittgenstein is himself committing the error attributed to Freud—neglecting important differences in reducing psychoanalytic interpretation to the genetic fallacy.[56]

Does the view of interpretations offered here avoid the criticism Wittgenstein made—that such statements are of the form "'This is *really* this"? After all, it might be objected, any dream interpretation, for example, depends upon a nonstandard understanding of some image. But then the interpretation involving such a nonstandard understanding seems to involve a claim like "This image (of an X) is *really* an image of a Y," which does seem to be of the form "This is *really* this" in Wittgenstein's eliminative sense.

Certainly, Freud often uses statements apparently of that form in interpreting dreams, for example. Thus, in describing one of his own dreams Freud writes, "in the dream I had replaced my patient by her friend."[57] Interpreting the same dream, he writes: "And now three similar situations came to my recollection involving my wife, Irma and the dead Mathilde. The identity of these situations had evidently enabled me to substitute the three figures for one another in the dream."[58] It is easy to suppose that the image of the person who seems to be Irma in the dream is actually an image of Freud's wife some of the time, and of the dead Mathilde at other times. Since the dream in question contained inconsistent, indeed mutually exclusive, explanations of his patient's pains, although all explanations agreed in exculpating himself, Freud sums up the interpretation by referring to "The whole plea—for the dream was nothing else."[59] Freud is committed to saying that the dream, which did not seem to him to be a plea prior to interpreting it, is really a plea.

56. The same confusion is to be found in Fisher and Greenberg's attribution to Freud of the view that the manifest content of a dream is a "meaningless shell" disguising the latent content (*Scientific Credibility of Freud's Theories and Therapy*, 23). For evidence that this attribution in incorrect, see Freud, *Interpretation of Dreams*, 4:163 and 277, for example; there, Freud seems to be thinking of the manifest content as meaningful.

57. Freud, *Interpretation of Dreams*, 4:110.

58. Ibid.

59. Ibid., 119–20.

To see why these and similar interpretive remarks do not genuinely exemplify the objectionable sort of statement Wittgenstein refers to as statements of the form "This is *really* this," it is necessary to recall that of course Wittgenstein does not object to the use of identity statements in general, for example, "The morning star is really the same heavenly body as the evening star." Only those identity statements that exemplify the genetic fallacy are meant to be rejected; that is, those that are of the form "(I) This is not really what it appears to be; it is really this, since this is what it is made of (or comes from, or can be reduced to)," which I shall call I-statements.

Psychoanalytic interpretations are not I-statements. There would be no occasion for an analyst to claim, for example, that a particular dream image was not really what it appeared to be an image of, but was instead an image of something else. The claim that a dream image, apparently of one thing, is really an image of something else instead must be distinguished from the claim that one dream image comes from (that is, is a condensation or displacement of) others. The difference is the same as that between the claim that a certain painted portrait apparently of one person is really a portrait of someone else, and the claim that a certain painted portrait was originally a portrait of someone else whose features the artist has partly or wholly painted over. Clearly, the two sets of claims must be kept apart; just as it may be true that fine scents are made of foul-smelling things, or that Redpath, like everyone else, leaves only a chemical residue when boiled, so, too, it may be true that one image in a dream originates in some other or others. The error comes when we imagine that these claims justify inferring that fine scents only appear to be fine and are really foul-smelling, that Redpath is something other than a real person, that the dream image is other than itself. The distinction needing to be preserved is that between statements of the form "This is really this," when these are eliminative, that is, when they are instances of the genetic fallacy, and identity statements that do not exemplify the genetic fallacy at all but that state, or claim to state, the nature of things: for example, "Lightning is really an electrical discharge." (If this last type of statement is reductive at all, it is not because it is an instance of the genetic fallacy that it is so.) That statements of the latter type are not essentially eliminative is clear from the fact that when true, such statements do not necessarily reduce the number of types of things a person can consistently believe to exist in the world. A viewer of lightning may wonder which of several things lightning really is — fire, sparks resulting from friction, or electricity. Telling such a person it is really an electrical discharge then has no eliminative force. The result is the same in the case of someone who has seen lightning but has no concept of electricity. Teaching such a person what electricity is and that lightning is really a form of it also has no eliminative force.

When Freud claims of a dream that it was really a plea, "and nothing else," is he making an I-statement?[60] Against this is the fact, as I have tried to show, that interpretations are not eliminative, whereas the reductive statements Wittgenstein properly objected to are; besides, Wittgenstein's objectionable statements are ones in which a thing's nature is identified with the materials out of which it arose or into which it can be turned, whereas Freud's statements are not. For if "It was really a plea" were an I-statement, its correctness would depend entirely upon the identification of the materials (bodily impressions during sleep, day's residues, childhood memories) from which the dream is supposed to have arisen. That Freud denied this is clear from his insistence upon unraveling the dream-work; that is, the processes that have been applied to the experiences from

60. The sense of (a) "The dream is a plea and nothing else" should not be confused with that of (b) "The dream is nothing but a plea" or (c) "The dream is nothing more than a plea." The meaning of (a) is ambiguous, since *else* is ambiguous (as the OED entry under that word explains). Thus, the question "Can I bring you something else?" can mean either "Can I bring you something *in addition* to what I have already brought?" or it can mean "Can I bring you something *in place of* what I have already brought?" Context alone determines what is meant. Analogously, (a) can mean (b) or (c), but it can also mean (d) "The dream is a plea, otherwise it is nothing." Now (b) and (c), which are not similarly ambiguous, are I-statements. By contrast, (a) is ambiguous, and so cannot be equivalent to (b) or (c). Therefore, the fact that (b) and (c) are I-statements does not imply that (a) is. In Freud's German, "Das ganze Plädoyer — nichts anderes ist dieser Traum," the word *anderes* is ambiguous in the same way that *else* is. Freud's meaning could be conveyed by translating these words as "The whole plea — for that is precisely what the dream was."

which the dream is claimed to have come; it is the dream-work that he identifies as the essence of the dream.[61] In short, however problematic it may be to assume a dream can even have an "underlying thought," making this assumption need not involve the genetic fallacy as Wittgenstein believed. Whatever independent problems interpretations may raise about their verification, their meaning is not necessarily the same as that of any I-statements.

Another feature of Wittgenstein's view of interpretations already referred to is closely related: his idea that interpretations are imposed on the patient. "One must have a very strong and keen and persistent criticism in order to recognize and see through the mythology that is offered or imposed on one. There is an inducement to say, 'Yes, of course, it must be like that.' A powerful mythology."[62] Clearly, no mere scaling-down of the aggressiveness of analysts in practice would remedy this situation. Wittgenstein's idea is that interpretations are essentially impositions, getting the patient to ignore differences, not see them. All the tentativeness, gentleness, in the world from analysts will not undo the imposition interpretations represent. Something of this worry about imposing comes out in the following remark:

> Many of these explanations are adopted because they have a peculiar charm. The picture of people having subconscious thoughts has a charm. The idea of an underworld, a secret cellar. Something hidden, uncanny. Cf. Keller's two children putting a live fly in the head of a doll, burying the doll and then running away.* (Why do we do this sort of thing? This is the sort of thing we do do.) A lot of things one is ready to believe because they are uncanny.

*Gottfried Keller (1819–1890). A Swiss poet, novelist and short-story writer. The incident to which Wittgenstein refers occurs in *Romeo und Julia auf dem Dorfe, Werke,* V–VI, Berlin, 1889, p. 84. Ed.[63]

61. Freud, *Interpretation of Dreams,* 5:506–7n. 2, 579–80n. 1; Freud, *The Ego and the Id,* 19:112.
62. Wittgenstein, *Lectures and Conversations,* 52.
63. Ibid., 25. The last sentence in the text (before the footnote) is slightly unclear; I assume Wittgenstein means "one is ready to believe many explanations because they are uncanny explanations — they make things appear

This is a very extreme sense of "imposing" — Wittgenstein assumes the interpretation, once offered, is accepted because it is charming; but no interpretation was felt necessary by the children in the example, whose behavior may seem uncanny to others. Here something different is involved in objecting to interpretation as imposed from what was meant before. For now it is not merely that interpretations persuade us to ignore differences; now interpretations persuade us that something needs to be interpreted to begin with. Interpretations are not felt necessary by those they are about, who also do not formulate them themselves. The impulse to interpret at all comes from outside the subject, hence the interpretation is imposed. "Consider the difficulty that if a symbol in a dream is not understood, it does not seem to be a symbol at all. So why call it one? But suppose I have a dream and accept a certain interpretation of it. *Then* — when I superimpose the interpretation on the dream — I can say 'Oh yes, the table obviously corresponds to the woman, this to that, etc.' "[64] Just how drastic a sense of imposition is involved here can be seen from the fact that no possible expansion of the practice of interpretation could overcome the force of interpretations as impositions. That is, suppose emphasis on infantile, sexual material was found too confining, and analysts sought to supplement or replace these with prospective interpretations, say, interpretations emphasizing emergent hopes, wishes, in dreams.[65] Such an "improvement" in technique would be utterly futile, from Wittgenstein's viewpoint, since "This is really a foreshadowing of that" is no less a form of persuasion, a mythology imposed upon the subject, than is "This is all a repetition of that." Trying to improve psychoanalytic interpretation in this way would be like trying to break out of a mythology seen to be defective, say Greek mythology, by adding to (or replacing it with) another, say, Norse myths! By the next year, 1943, Wittgenstein came to see that

---

uncanny." Taken this way, he is repeating what the first quoted sentence says.

64. Ibid., 44.

65. For such an expansion, see Erikson, "Nature of Clinical Evidence"; and Erikson, "Dream Specimen of Psychoanalysis."

there is something wrong with the view of interpretations as impositions, in the sense that no need for an interpretation is even felt by the subject prior to the interpretation being offered: "It is characteristic of dreams that often they seem to the dreamer to call for an interpretation. One is hardly ever inclined to write down a day dream, or recount it to someone else, or to ask 'What does it mean?' But dreams do seem to have something puzzling and in a special way interesting about them — so that we want an interpretation of them. (They were often regarded as messages.)"[66] If Wittgenstein is to continue to claim that interpretations essentially persuade us to ignore differences, he must cope with a fairly obvious objection — that Freud derives his interpretations from the patient's own free associations. Freud expects the significance of the parts of the dream to be revealed through the patient's own free associations to them. Such a method does not seem to involve imposing upon the patient in any sense, if the method is what Freud takes it to be.

> The technique which I describe in the pages that follow differs in one essential respect from the ancient method: it imposes the task of interpretation upon the dreamer himself. It is not concerned with what occurs to the *interpreter* in connection with a particular element of the dream, but with what occurs to the dreamer . . . the work of the interpretation is not brought to bear on the dream as a whole, but on each portion of the dream's content independently, as though the dream were a geological conglomerate in which each fragment of rock required a separate assessment.[67]

The final portions of Wittgenstein's "Conversations on Freud" are concerned, in part, with showing that the technique need not be taken as Freud does, that the dream and its associations are not related as Freud supposes.[68] Wittgenstein seeks to undermine the idea that the dream's essence is revealed in the process of interpretation, that dreams and their free associations are meaningfully connected to dream-thoughts, as Freud supposed.

66. Wittgenstein, *Lectures and Conversations,* 45.
67. Freud, *Interpretation of Dreams,* 4:98n. 1, and 99.
68. Wittgenstein, *Lectures and Conversations,* 45–52.

> When a dream is interpreted we might say that it is fitted into a context in which it ceases to be puzzling. In a sense the dreamer re-dreams his dream in surroundings such that its aspect changes. It is as though we were presented with a bit of canvas on which were painted a hand and a part of a face and certain other shapes, arranged in a puzzling and incongruous manner. Suppose this bit is surrounded by considerable stretches of blank canvas, and that we now paint in forms—say an arm, a trunk, etc.— leading up to and fitting on to the shapes on the original bit; and that the result is that we say: "Ah, now I see why it is like that, how it all comes to be arranged in that way, and what these various bits are . . ." and so on.[69]

This is the first of several models of dream interpretation Wittgenstein imagines to bring out the point. Here, when the dreamer free-associates to the dream's elements, "the dreamer re-dreams his dream"; the free associations therefore have the same status as more dream material and need not be taken as revealing anything deeper about the dream. Here is another such model:

> Suppose we were to regard a dream as a kind of game which the dreamer played. . . . There might be a game in which paper figures were put together to form a story, or at any rate were somehow assembled. The materials might be collected and stored in a scrap-book, full of pictures and anecdotes. The child might then take various bits from the scrap-book to put into the construction; and he might take a considerable picture because it had something in it which he wanted and he might just include the rest because it was there.[70]

Of course, even if it is assumed that some features of the manifest dream or of the associations to it need not signify anything about the latent dream, that is, may be there simply because they are connected with things that do signify, the point is critical of Freud's method only if it is impossible to distinguish between the two sorts of features, that is, between an element having "something in it which he wanted" and "the rest [included] because it was there." The distinction is needed and can be made in the two models only because it is presumably a rule of the game in both models that one

69. Ibid., 45–46.
70. Ibid., 49–50.

may not cut the elements provided (bits of canvas, materials in the scrapbook) into pieces; but such a rule does not seem to be at work in dreaming, where condensation and displacement are assumed to be the norm. In the games, the distinction collapses if it is assumed that players may cut the games' elements at will. Wittgenstein carries his view of free associations as arbitrarily related to the dream whose interpretation they are supposed to be essential to, to fantastic, though logical, conclusions: "If I take any one of the dream reports (reports of his own dreams) which Freud gives, I can by the use of free association arrive at the same results as those he reaches in his analysis — although it was not my dream. And the association will proceed through my own experiences and so on."[71] Wittgenstein is right to say that his (or anyone's) free associations would lead to the same interpretation of *some* dream elements as the dreamer's associations — especially in the case of elements having sexual significance. But that anyone's associations would arrive at the same results as the dreamer's in all respects is implausible.[72] The truth of this claim need not concern us; more interesting is what it reveals about the first two models of dream interpretation and why they are poor models. The "puzzling shapes" in the first, the "bits from the scrapbook" in the second, do not originate with the person who elaborates them. By contrast, the dream elements for free association do originate with the interpreter. Another way in which Wittgenstein's analogues to dream interpretation fail is suggested when he writes: "You could start with any of the objects on this table — which certainly are not put there through your dream activity — and you could find that they all could be connected in a pattern like that; and the pattern would be logical in the same way."[73] However, there is not normally anything puzzling about the arrangement of objects on a table, or even any reason to assume one person placed them all there. But a dream is necessarily the product of one person's mind and is

71. Ibid., 50.
72. For an example in which Freud makes the distinction, see Freud, *Interpretation of Dreams* (dream IV), 4:269–71. The whole discussion of "typical" dreams (241–78) is relevant.
73. Wittgenstein, *Lectures and Conversations*, 51.

inherently puzzling, as Wittgenstein conceded. In none of his models do the elements of the play seem to mean anything before the processes analogous to free association are attempted. In the first, Wittgenstein says the shapes are arranged in a puzzling and incongruous manner; but it is hard to see why it is puzzling, unless one person is assumed to have arranged them all with the intention of depicting something. Then the puzzle is to determine what that person meant to depict.

These differences between Wittgenstein's models and the actual activity of dream interpretation are significant. In each, arbitrary aspects of the game and the elements it is played with are built in by virtue of features necessarily not present to begin with in the case of dream interpretation. Yet the analogies are supposed to bring out the arbitrary relation between dream and free associations. We can convert even the last, most implausible, of Wittgenstein's models into a case involving nonarbitrary relatedness by eliminating the two features noted. Thus, in the fourth model, suppose one person did put all the objects on the table (for one or various purposes) and is the same person free-associating to them. It would then be plausible to expect the associations to point to the reason (or reasons) for putting them there, to remind the person if the reason has been forgotten. So the features of Wittgenstein's four examples that render the free association analogues in them arbitrarily related to the dream analogues in them are features that must be absent from any genuine case of free association to a dream in Freud's sense.[74]

FREUD AND THE WITTGENSTEIN OF THE *TRACTATUS* COMPARED

What might have provoked Wittgenstein in the idea of an essentially meaningful connection between free associations to ele-

---

74. I have restricted myself here to reasons for rejecting Wittgenstein's intentionally subversive models of the relation between free associations and dream-thoughts as Freud conceived it. Wittgenstein's skepticism is anticipated by Freud (*Interpretation of Dreams*, 5:527) and rejected (ibid., 527–32).

ments in dreams and "dream-thoughts" is the resemblance of this idea to his own earlier *Tractatus* views, which he had rejected by the time these remarks were made. For Freud, a dream is a disguised representation of a latent thought; free association is meant to bring us from the former to the latter. Similarly, Wittgenstein had treated the proposition as a disguised picture that is essentially connected with the situation it depicts;[75] analysis derives the latter from the former.[76] For Wittgenstein, the proposition and the situation it represents must have the same logical multiplicity.[77] Similarly, Freud writes that the dream content is expressed as if "in a pictographic script the characters of which have to be transposed individually into the language of the dream-thoughts."[78]

Wittgenstein sees Freud as committed to a vain search for the essence of dreaming—the structure all dreams must share;[79] whereas he insisted that no one such thing need exist.[80] Wittgenstein himself had deduced the essence of the significant proposition in the *Tractatus* but had later come to see such a unifying feature as illusory.[81] But if Freud's conception of dream-analysis is rejected because of its similarity to Wittgenstein's *Tractatus* conception of the analysis of propositions, it is arguable that the analogy has been pressed beyond its proper limits. For Wittgenstein's argument is wholly a priori—if a proposition is to have meaning, it must picture a situation. But Freud's account of the relation between manifest dream and latent dream-thought is based on no such necessity. So the failure of the a priori argument in no way implies the failure of Freud's claim to have discovered the common structure of dreams; there may well be one.

The claim to have discovered something essential about dreams (or anything else) need not be pernicious, although such claims be-

75. Wittgenstein, *Tractatus*, 4.01, 4.011, 4.03; see also 4.014, 4.016.
76. Ibid., 3.2, 3.201, 3.25.
77. Ibid., 4.04.
78. Freud, *Interpretation of Dreams*, 4:277.
79. Wittgenstein, *Lectures and Conversations*, 48.
80. Ibid., 50.
81. Wittgenstein, *Blue Book*, 17ff.; *Philosophical Investigations*, paragraph 23.

come so when they imply completeness — when they are taken as characterizations of the whole of a thing's essence, that is, as implying there is nothing more to the thing. Wittgenstein's picture theory of the proposition is of that type; as he wrote in the *Tractatus*, "3.25 A proposition has one and only one complete analysis." Wittgenstein seems to have assumed Freud was thinking along similar lines:

> Freud seems to have certain prejudices about when an interpretation could be regarded as complete — and so about when it still requires completion, when further interpretation is needed. Suppose someone were ignorant of the tradition among sculptors of making busts. If he then came upon the finished bust of some man, he might say that obviously this is a fragment and that there must have been other parts belonging to it, making it a whole body.
>
> Suppose you recognized certain things in the dream which can be interpreted in the Freudian manner. Is there any ground at all for assuming that there must be an interpretation for everything else in the dream as well? that it makes any sense to ask what is the right interpretation of the other things there?[82]

Yet Freud was emphatic that "dreams, like all other psychopathological structures, regularly have more than one meaning. . . . It is in fact never possible to be sure that a dream has been completely interpreted."[83] Implications of the analogy are wrong for what Wittgenstein means; he speaks as if he had a criterion for completeness (the "finished bust of some man"), one Freud had exceeded. But Wittgenstein had no such criterion in the case of dreams, and he means to cast doubt on there being one to find, just as Freud had said. Of course, Wittgenstein's point is that Freud finds too much meaning in the manifest dream, not all of it need have meaning. But the meanings Freud finds do not result from the insistence in advance that everything in a dream must have meaning; Freud merely reports on the abundance of meanings spontaneously arising, once the dreamer's free associations are brought into play. And he regards it as evidence of the power of the technique that it finds meaning in

82. Wittgenstein, *Lectures and Conversations*, 49.
83. Freud, *Interpretation of Dreams*, 4:149, 279.

elements of the dream that do not at first seem to have meaning, even when others do. Freud's view of the essence of dreams differs from Wittgenstein's view of the essence of the proposition in that the latter claims completeness in a way that the former does not. Wittgenstein does not appear to have noticed this difference.

Perhaps because of this difference, although the flow of Freud's thought after *The Interpretation of Dreams* roughly parallels that of Wittgenstein's post-*Tractatus* views, Freud did not have to repudiate his earlier ideas, whereas Wittgenstein did find it necessary. Wittgenstein rejected the idea of the proposition as picture in favor of finding the proposition's meaning in its use in language games; Freud shifts emphasis from a view of symptoms as depictions of unconscious processes, to one in which their defensive function for the ego is uppermost. But Freud never entirely gave up his earlier ideas.

For Freud, the essence of dreaming is the dream-work — those condensations and displacements (among other things) by which manifest dreams are produced from censored material.[84] Such work need not always be inferred about the past, as is the case with dreams; mental activity of that sort can also be observed in the present in the patient's responses to the analyst. There, in the patient's relation to the analyst, the distortions and misconceptions of the analyst's thoughts and feelings can be observed in direct contact with those thoughts and feelings themselves. This might be compared to witnessing a dream being fashioned — where the analyst is the analogue of the latent dream-thoughts and thus knows what is being distorted. Treated as repetitions of infantile prototypes, such transference phenomena are categorically superior to dreams or symptoms as evidence of the contents of the unconscious, Freud held. Whereas dreams or symptoms are representations of such prototypes, the transference gives the analyst the thing itself. Thus, Freud writes of the phenomena of transference as "making the patient's hidden and forgotten erotic impulses immediate and manifest. For when all is said and done, it is impossible to destroy anyone *in absentia* or *in effigie*."[85] To be destroyed are the "prototypes" or

84. Ibid., 506n. 2, 507.
85. Freud, "Dynamics of Transference," 108.

"stereotype plates,"[86] "infantile stereotypes"[87] that are repeated in the transference, not disguised as in dreams or symptoms and that are comparable to "effigies."[88] "The patient repeats these modes of reaction during the work of analysis. . . . He produces them before our eyes, as it were. In fact, it is only in this way that we get to know them."[89] Based on such remarks, a three-tiered hierarchy of types of interpretations can be constructed: (1) interpretations ascribing unconscious content (for example, of dreams, jokes, symptoms) for which there are no criteria entirely independent of the subject's assent; (2) interpretations of defenses/resistances, for which criteria more or less independent of the subject's assent exist, but which do not necessarily determine what unconscious ideas are being resisted or defended against; (3) interpretations of the transference, for which criteria independent of the subject's assent exist, and which do ascribe unconscious content to the subject, that is, which do determine what unconscious ideas are being resisted or defended against.

Of course, none of this implies that interpreting the transference is easier than interpreting dreams or symptoms or defenses. On the contrary, transference interpretations depend upon and incorporate symptom and defense interpretations.

ARE PSYCHOANALYTIC INTERPRETATIONS MEANINGLESS?

In the end, Wittgenstein's response to the claim of analysis that it can, through interpretation, uncover the truth about certain very particular human problems appears to have been mixed; in a conversation with Rush Rhees in 1942 he remarked, "There is no way of showing that the whole result of analysis may not be 'delusion.' It is something which people are inclined to accept and which makes it easier for them to go certain ways."[90] Yet a private note-

---

86. Ibid., 100.
87. Freud, "Observations on Transference-Love," 12:168.
88. Freud, "Analysis Terminable and Interminable," 23:238.
89. Ibid.
90. Wittgenstein, *Lectures and Conversations*, 44.

book entry from 1939 appears to assert the exact opposite: "In a way having oneself psychoanalyzed is like eating from the tree of knowledge. The knowledge acquired sets us (new) ethical problems; but contributes nothing to their solution."[91] It is unclear at first how the result of analysis can be both knowledge, which makes it harder to continue, and also delusion, which makes it easier. Eating the fruit of the tree in question gives knowledge of good and evil, however; B. McGuinness notes, after quoting the 1939 entry, that "Wittgenstein was inclined to think that the chief good it [analysis] would do them [friends and relations] would reside in the shame they were bound to feel at all the things they would have to reveal to their analyst."[92] So, for Wittgenstein, the knowledge gained from analysis has nothing to do with *its* truth, and the "certain ways" analysis makes it easier to go do not involve the solution of the ethical problems such knowledge raises or even the pursuit of those solutions. Thus, the 1939 notebook entry and the 1942 quote are not really opposed. But could the result of psychoanalytic inquiry be "delusion"? A delusion is a false belief, one "maintained in spite of argument, data and refutation which should (reasonably) be sufficient to destroy it."[93] So in claiming that the results of psychoanalytic inquiry might be delusion, Wittgenstein stops far short of claiming that those results are meaningless. That more extreme view has been expounded by Frank Cioffi, though using arguments derived from Wittgenstein:

> In one of his dream interpretations Freud advances the claim that the red, camellia-shaped blossoms which his patient reported carrying were "an unmistakable allusion to menstruation" and supports this by reference to La Dame aux Camelias who signalled the onset of her menstrual periods by replacing her usual white camellia with a red one [Freud, *Interpretation of Dreams*, 4:319]. Though we can give a sense to the statement that the dream blossoms owed their shape and colour to the dreamer's familiarity with "La Dame aux Camelias," and that if menstrual blood were

91. Wittgenstein, *Culture and Value,* 34; quoted and discussed in McGuinness, "Freud and Wittgenstein," 28–29.
92. McGuinness, "Freud and Wittgenstein," 29.
93. Reber, *Penguin Dictionary of Psychology,* 184.

green, they too would have been green, it is not the sense which Freud requires, for it is not the kind of thing to which the dreamer could attest. She might agree but she could not corroborate.[94]

For Cioffi, there is no problem in asserting a causal relation between the color of the blossoms in the dream and the color of the blossoms as used by La Dame aux Camelias in the fiction familiar to the dreamer; "we can give a sense to" such a causal claim, he says. What cannot be done is to treat as *corroboration* the dreamer's acceptance of Freud's claim that the dream-blossoms *allude* to the fictional ones. Certainly, if the interpretation is analyzed to be of the form "This dream-image is really this," Cioffi's claim would be correct. After all, how could the dreamer's assent have any special role in assessing a statement of that sort, whatever that sort of statement can be supposed to mean? But if the interpretation is of the form "This dream says 'this is really that,'" then the dreamer's assent is convincing prima facie evidence that that is what it says. That Cioffi does think of interpretations just as Wittgenstein did, namely, as of the form "This is *really* this" is clear in an earlier essay, where he writes, "Freud certainly produced statements to which an enormous number of people have said 'yes,' but there are good grounds for assimilating his achievement to that of the anonymous geniuses to whom it first occurred that Tuesday is lean and Wednesday fat, the low notes on the piano dark and the high notes light. Except that instead of words, notes and shades, we have scenes from human life."[95] A natural objection is that in dream interpretation, unlike in these cases, evidence relevant to the truth of the interpretations exists apart from the mere assent of the dreamer — in the dreamer's free associations to the elements of the dream. Roughly, if and when the associations to each element taken separately converge towards an interpretation, then the interpretation has been confirmed to some degree, even before it has been offered to the subject. Even if the dreamer's assent is the criterion of correctness, such convergence

94. Cioffi, "Freud and the Idea of a Pseudo-Science," 496. (I have updated Cioffi's reference to the passage from Freud.)

95. Cioffi, "Wittgenstein's Freud," 209–10.

in associations is relevant to predicting what interpretations the dreamer will assent to. Thus, even if the interpretation is treated as nothing more than a prediction of what will be assented to by the dreamer, there may be good grounds justifying the interpreter's offering it. But the question of whether free association might approximate what a dream-element alludes to can arise only if it is assumed that such allusion is possible, an assumption Cioffi rejects; so, of course, free association as evidence of such allusion must be rejected, too. "Freud contrives by the use of such idioms as 'allusion' to get us to assimilate his explananda to a class of actions and reactions, enquiry into which naturally terminates in our receipt of the agent-subject's account of the matter, e.g., the course taken by his thoughts during a brown study."[96] Cioffi's identification of a dreamer's free associations with "the course taken by his thoughts during a brown study" is confused, since a brown study is "an idle or purposeless reverie," a daydream,[97] whereas free association is none of these things. First of all, in free association one speaks one's thoughts, suspending self-censorship, aware that another is listening; attention must be paid to ensure that normal constraints of discourse are not permitted to operate.[98] But that someone is speaking, aware, and attending in those ways at all argues against that person being in a reverie or daydream. In free-associating to the elements in a dream, the items in the dream whose meaning is sought must be attended to in isolation from the others. In free association the subject pursues some assumed meaning by attending to "sudden ideas," "eruptions" in thought, which pass without notice in a reverie.[99] These confusions about the nature of free association undermine Cioffi's claim

96. Cioffi, "Freud and the Idea of a Pseudo-Science," 496.
97. *Oxford English Dictionary* entries under *brown study* and *reverie*.
98. Freud, "Two Encyclopedia Articles," 18:238.
99. Cioffi may have been misled by the term *free association*, a dubious translation of Freud's "freier Einfall" that has become standard in English. See the editor's note at Freud, *Introductory Lectures on Psycho-Analysis*, 15:47–48, as well as entries under "free association" in Laplanche and Pontalis's *Language of Psychoanalysis*, and Moore and Fine, eds., *Psychoanalytic Terms and Concepts*.

that "whatever Pyramidologists are doing when they discover allusions to mathematical and scientific truths in the dimensions of the Great Pyramid. . . . It is this which Freud is doing when he 'lays bare' the secret significance of his patients' dreams, symptoms, errors, memories and associations."[100] The lack of analogy between Pyramidology and psychoanalytic interpretation comes out in a quote Cioffi provides from Martin Gardner:

> It is not difficult to understand how [Pyramidologists] achieved these astonishing scientific correspondences. If you set about measuring a complicated structure like the Pyramid, you will quickly have on hand a great abundance of lengths to play with. If you have sufficient patience to juggle them about in various ways, you are certain to come out with many figures which coincide with important figures in the sciences. Since you are bound by no rules, it would be odd indeed if this search for Pyramid 'truths' failed to meet with considerable success.
>
> Take the Pyramid's height, for example. Smyth multiplies it by ten to the ninth power to obtain the distance to the sun. The nine here is purely arbitrary. And if no simple multiple had yielded the distance to the sun, he could try other multiples to see if it gave the distance to the moon, or the nearest star, or any other scientific figure.[101]

Unlike the elements of a dream, however, which are all dreamt by one human subject, the distance between earth and sun and the Pyramid's height were not produced by the same person — indeed, the former was not produced by a human being at all. In addition, there is no independent evidence that Egyptian builders knew the distance between earth and sun or thought it relevant to pyramid construction, whereas the dreamer engaged in free association believes that the dream means something, that the elements in the dream are related, that it is about something.[102] Lastly, there is no

---

100. Cioffi, "Freud and the Idea of a Pseudo-Science," 498.

101. Martin Gardner, cited ibid., 491.

102. Indeed, such beliefs are not peculiar to practitioners of free association: "Dreams everywhere and always have been seen as somehow significant and meaningful," according to G. W. Domhoff (*Mystique of Dreams*, 2); "Dream *interpretation* is a cultural universal," writes Barbara Tedlock (*Dreaming*, ix).

convergence to a common historical cause to be found between the height of the pyramid and the distance between sun and earth, whereas convergence is found when free association is employed on the elements of a dream.

In order to arrive at convergence, must the person associating be the dreamer? If plausible interpretations can be reached by free associating to random assortments of items in reality, or to another person's dream, then convergence would count for little in support of the method of free association. Cioffi replies to the claim that convergence is evidence that interpretations are not merely the result of ingenuity in exploiting the inevitable coincidences to be found in any materials:

> Wittgenstein doubts this: "Freud remarks on how after the analysis of it, the dream appears so very logical. And of course it does. You could start with any of the objects on this table — which certainly were not put there by your dream activity — and you could find that they all could be connected in a pattern like that, and the pattern would be logical in the same way."*
>
> Either Wittgenstein's table was more cluttered than mine or he shared Freud's genius for constructing associative links between any two points, for I have not been able to produce patterns anywhere near as convincing as Freud's. But the force of this consideration is weakened if we remember that Freud lays his own table: "The material belonging to a single subject can only be collected piece by piece at various times and in various connexions."
>
> But it is the elasticity and multiplicity of the rules which do most to reduce the *a priori* improbability of producing associative links to and between his patients' dreams, symptoms, reminiscences, etc., where there are really none.

> *Barrett, *Lectures and Conversations,* p. 51.[103]

There are three problems with this reply. First, Cioffi's admission of failure in connecting indicates that the presence or absence of degrees of convergence is at least roughly testable. Second, Cioffi's defense that "Freud lays his own table" — that is, selects material to

103. Cioffi, "Wittgenstein's Freud," 203.

interpret from a person's whole life — will not do for the sort of case Wittgenstein addresses, namely dream interpretation. Given a dream as reported in words by the dreamer, convergence in the dreamer's associations occurs even when analysis of the dreamer's life history is not in question. Then, the interpreter has little opportunity to "lay his own table." Cioffi's point here would be plausible only if the analysis of a subject's whole life history were at issue. But convergence is to be found when single dreams are subjected to the dreamer's free associations, more so than when association is applied to randomly selected objects in reality. Third, Cioffi's last quoted sentence about "associative links" is at least very ambiguous; the analyst, it seems, produces them, so they are not the associations of the patient, they are interpretations. But then Cioffi says of such associative links that "(i) there are really none there." What can the criterion be, according to which there really are no links, whether associations by the patient or interpretations by the analyst is understood? After all, one would suppose that interpretations or associations exist if analysts or patients produce them. It is hard to avoid the impression here that by "associative links" Cioffi means relations linking dreams and symptoms considered in themselves, apart from the associations of the dreamer or the interpretations of the analyst. It is as if Cioffi supposes some means is available for inspecting dreams and symptoms in themselves; in addition to the associations and interpretations, Cioffi thinks we can also observe the presence or absence of links in reality between symptoms and dreams, associations and interpretations.

Now opposition to such a view need not be based, as may at first appear, on the conception of the dream as a private object, accessible only to the dreamer, so that only the dreamer can inspect the dream in itself. Even if we define dreams by the narratives given by dreamers, it is not obvious what criterion can be applied to show that dreams, symptoms, interpretations really are without the links analysts find and dreamers and patients accept. Cioffi seems here to have fallen under the spell of his own (and Wittgenstein's) comparison; of objects on a table we can say, as an empirical fact, that there really is no meaning to their being there. We might guarantee this by having a different person choose each item without knowing what the others have chosen. Then, if someone finds "associative links" among the objects, we know they are projecting such links onto the objects, much as a subject responding to a Rorschach inkblot does. We know that none of the "associative links" are really there. But dreams are different; one person is known to have produced the dream, and the dream often seems meaningful to the dreamer, before the dreamer has even heard of psychoanalysis.[104] We are not in a position here to say that the dream is really not meaningful, as a testable fact, the way we are with the inkblot or random objects on a table.

Another unclarity in understanding (i) depends on the same point; if Cioffi means that Freud produced "associative links" where there are no such links, one implication of this might be that although dreams, symptoms, and so on are often really linked in such ways, Freud says that such links exist in certain cases where there really are none. This would commit Cioffi to saying that "associative links" are really there to be found, that he knows what it would be like to find them in dreams, and so on — but then Freud is merely being criticized as a clumsy or overzealous interpreter, while the method of analysis itself, that is, the making of "associative links," remains unproblematic. On the other hand, Cioffi might mean that there really are never any "associative links" between dreams, symptoms, free associations, and so on. Saying this would be compatible with either of two claims: (a) that dreams have meanings but that Freud's method of "associative links" never gets at them; or (b) that dreams have no meaning at all. What Cioffi has in mind seems to be (b), since this way of reading (i) conforms more closely to his later writing:

104. The importance of this second condition for the hypothesis of the meaningfulness of dreams can be seen from the near impossibility of introducing the idea that dreams have meaning into a world in which people report dreams but (a) never interpret their own dreams; (b) never assent to interpretations offered by others; (c) never think their own dreams are meaningful; and (d) never free-associate. In such a world, interpreting the meaning of dreams would be like interpreting inkblots or the random arrangements of objects on a table.

Our descent into unintelligibility is, on most occasions, concealed from us by the gentleness of the declivity, the succession of subtle dislocations of sense to which the idioms in which the interpretations have been couched were subjected. To free ourselves we have to make explicit the tacitly performed assimilations which produce the illusion of intelligibility and hide from us the extent to which the absence of the normal surroundings deprives Freud's interpretations of sense.[105]

If Cioffi thought dreams had meaning that Freud's interpretations failed to capture, he would not say that Freud's interpretations lacked sense; he would say they were wrong, untrue. This way of reading (i) also seems to be implied when Cioffi writes, "We did not interpret dreams, symptoms, errors, etc., because it was discovered that they were meaningful, but we insisted that they were meaningful in order that we might interpret them. And if we reflect on the kind of evidence it involves, we will not find it surprising that it should prove incapable of demonstration and give rise to intractable disagreement, for it is not a question of proving of some isolated thesis of psychoanalysis that it fails to meet a particular criterion but of discerning a pattern in the total ensemble."[106] Here, Cioffi means to say either (c) dreams, symptoms, errors are really meaningless, or (d) dreams and so on have meaning, but only because we insist they do, not because we have discovered this. Now (d) borders on absurdity, for it is hard to see how anything can acquire meaning simply by having some people insist it has it. However, Cioffi has not provided any arguments to support (c), which is not surprising, since the task of proving (c) might be compared to that of persuading poets and literary critics that all poetry is meaningless, or religious people that all rituals are meaningless. Cioffi would need to provide a theory of meaning to justify such extreme claims, but as we shall see, such a theory would require rejecting considerable portions of his own views. The claim that there really are no "associative links," that is, (i), would make sense if interpretations were thought of as the analyst's free associations to the patient's dreams, symptoms, and so on; but then the claim would still be false. Maintaining that

---

105. Cioffi, "Freud and the Idea of a Pseudo-Science," 497.
106. Ibid., 497.

(i) is true would also be meaningful if the statements asserting that such links exist were thought of as having the form "This is *really* this"; then Cioffi would be denying that such claims are ever true. Since such claims are never psychoanalytic interpretations, Cioffi would not have refuted Freud, even if we agree that in this sense, there really are no "associative links." It is especially doubtful that this second way of reading (i) — that is, as entailing (b) and (c) above — can be made consistent with another claim of Cioffi's: "It is fair to conclude that though the introduction of the term 'libido' permits Freud to give the impression that claims are being advanced as to the nature of the vicissitudes which precipitate, or the states which predispose to, the development of neurotic disorders, in fact a convention has been adopted as to how these vicissitudes and states are to be described."[107] For it is hard to see what descriptions that convention can authorize on the second reading of (i); since no description of what any dream or symptom means (involving reference to libido, for example) is ever true, there ought to be nothing for the convention Cioffi writes of to authorize.

The difficulties raised here about Cioffi's remarks about meaning come to the fore when he criticizes Freud for writing of the blossoms in the dream discussed earlier as "an unmistakable allusion to menstruation," for example, "Consider the term 'allusion.' It is typically used [by Freud] short of its full force, in a strained sense, like that in which one might say that a hangover is an allusion to alcoholic overindulgence or a winter sun-tan to a Mediterranean holiday."[108] Cioffi's concession that one might say of a hangover that it is an allusion "in a strained sense" to alcoholic overindulgence is a red herring; ordinarily, hangovers are not allusions to anything in any sense, strained or otherwise, since they do not playfully refer to or symbolize anything. Unusual cases in which one person drinks excessively in order to become hung over so as to allude to another's alcoholic overindulgence in their presence are cases in which a hangover is an allusion, but not in any strained sense; so too is the case of the secret alcoholic who has thus far carefully avoided allowing

107. Ibid., 477.
108. Ibid., 496.

friends to see him hung over, but who now intentionally creates a situation in which for the first time they will see him so. Here, the drinker's hangover alludes to his own alcoholic overindulgence, again, in a sense which is in no way strained. (Parallel considerations apply to winter suntans, though perhaps cases in which they allude are more common than those in which hangovers do.) Thus, Freud's use of allusion is not strained; the woman's dream of herself carrying blossoms might be an allusion to menstruation just as carrying blossoms in a play or pageant might; there is nothing strained about it in either case. Of course, what someone is alluding to in saying or doing something may not be clear to us, even though we may be certain that an allusion to something has been made. The phenomenon giving Cioffi trouble is not specific to psychoanalytic interpretation — it is the kind of difficulty involved when we inquire what some particular person meant by saying or doing a certain thing at a specific time and place, as opposed to the meanings of words and sentences more or less independent of those considerations, for example, when we ask what someone meant or was alluding to in telling a particular joke at a funeral. The meanings of the words used as given in the dictionary and the sentences they make up are not what puzzle us, nor have we failed to grasp that a joke was being told, that is, that what was said was supposed to be funny, and perhaps even that it was funny. These are presupposed as understood by joker and questioners alike; otherwise, they could not even be puzzled by the joke, or by the telling of it then and there. The puzzle concerns what the telling of the joke *meant* to the teller and its hearers. It would be a mistake to suppose that the meaning of the joke, that particular joke, then and there, could be worked out in accordance with much more complex rules of the same sort as are used to determine the meaning of the individual words and sentences uttered in telling it. Hence the suspect nature of Cioffi's reference to the "elasticity and multiplicity of the rules" Freud is supposed to employ in interpretation.[109] Presumably, what the telling of the joke meant is determined by the joker telling us, or assenting to an interpretation, though other evidence is certainly possible. Cases in

109. Cioffi, "Wittgenstein's Freud," 203.

which people do not know why they say or think certain things — in which the things they say or think seem alien to them — do not introduce new senses of "meaning" or "allusion" or strain the senses of these terms, as Cioffi supposes. Such cases do bring out the limitations of his theory of meaning. That Cioffi has no coherent account of meaning capable of encompassing the various things he himself says about interpretations is clear from the fact that, while much of the time he claims interpretations are meaningless, at other times he appears to protect their sense, however limited he might think it is. Thus, he compares interpretations to statements such as "Tuesday is lean, Wednesday is fat" — which is whimsical, but not meaningless; produces associative patterns linking objects on a table, but says of his patterns that they are not "as convincing as Freud's" (or Wittgenstein's), which implies genuine conviction in such pattern-production is possible; and even compares psychoanalytic interpretation to great literature, as when he writes, "In *La Vita Nuova,* Dante argues that the date of Beatrice's death, 9 June 1290, was determined by her relation to the Trinity and other significant numerical values. . . . Whatever Dante was doing when he found a trinitarian allusion in the date of Beatrice's death . . . Freud is doing when he 'lays bare' the secret significance of his patients' dreams."[110] Cioffi's dilemma on this point is probably inevitable as long as interpretations are represented as spinning webs of pseudo-meaning, "spurious allusions"[111] about essentially meaningless entities such as dreams and symptoms. For on that representation, how can the claim that dreams are essentially meaningless be justified (that is, tested), without pretending to the kind of knowledge about what dreams are like when laid bare that Freud is being criticized for supposedly claiming to possess?

Just how far Cioffi's idea that dreams are really meaningless is from anything Wittgenstein had in mind can be gauged from a note Wittgenstein wrote in 1948:

> In Freudian analysis a dream is dismantled, as it were. It loses its original sense *completely.* . . . What is intriguing about a dream is not its *causal*

110. Cioffi, "Freud and the Idea of a Pseudo-Science," 490, 498.
111. Ibid., 491.

connection with events in my life, etc., but rather the impression it gives of being a fragment of a story — a very *vivid* fragment to be sure — the rest of which remains obscure. (We feel like asking: "where did this figure come from then and what became of it?") What's more, if someone now shows me that this story is not the right one; that in reality it was based on a quite different story, so that I want to exclaim disappointedly "Oh, *that's* how it was?", it really is as though I have been deprived of something. . . . It can certainly be said that contemplation of the dream-image inspires us, that we just *are* inspired. Because if we tell someone else our dream the image will not usually inspire him. The dream affects us as does an idea pregnant with possible developments.[112]

What disappoints Wittgenstein is the loss (as he sees it) of the dream's sense when psychoanalytic interpretation is applied to it; whereas Cioffi attacks the finding of any sense at all in dreams. Against both, I have tried to show that there is nothing unreasonable about ascribing meaning to dreams and that no dismantling of the sense of a dream, no reduction of the dream's possible developments, occurs in psychoanalytic interpretation.

Sense cannot be made of psychoanalytic interpretation apart from the psychoanalytic conception of the unconscious, and an understanding of the unconscious is not possible apart from the view of resistance (and of transference) phenomena peculiar to it, according to Freud. Our next task, then, is to understand what Freud meant by resistance and what the connection is between resistance and the unconscious. Why is the psychoanalytic unconscious dependent on the phenomenon of resistance for its sense, and why does the absence of resistance make attributions of unconscious mental activity problematic? These questions will be explored in chapter 2.

112. Wittgenstein, *Culture and Value*, 68–69. Wittgenstein's own view of dreams here, as before, is similar in some ways to Carl Jung's in such works as *Psychology and Religion* (1938), where Jung writes, "He [Freud] explains the dream as a mere façade, behind which something has been carefully hidden" (30) and doubts "whether we can assume that a dream is something else than it appears to be" (30–31). As footnote 56 above indicates, Jung, like Wittgenstein and Fisher and Greenberg, has misunderstood Freud on this point.

2

Is the Psychoanalytic Unconscious a Dispensable Concept?

The best way to focus on the nature of resistance, which was central to Freud's conception of unconscious mental activity, is to examine arguments for and against the existence of unconscious mental activity in which the element of resistance is lacking. Paradoxically, one of Freud's favorite arguments in support of unconscious mental activity — that is, the argument from posthypnotic suggestion — is an example of the first. James's very influential attempted refutation of the idea of unconscious mental activity in *The Principles of Psychology* illustrates the second. After examining these, I conclude this chapter with an account of the idea of resistance drawn from what I take to be the failure of all of these arguments.

FREUD'S POSTHYPNOTIC SUGGESTION ARGUMENT

When confronted with doubts about the existence of unconscious mental activity, Freud would reply with two sorts of arguments, the first of which he based on the phenomenon of posthypnotic suggestion. He tended to employ this argument when explaining his views to nonpsychoanalysts and beginners in analysis, perhaps just because it seems to establish his fundamental concept without appealing to any of the distinctive clinical data familiar to practitioners of psychoanalysis.[1] One implication of this argument's independence from psychoanalysis is that the psychoanalytic concept of the unconscious will not be undermined if the argument fails. This needs to be emphasized because the first task of this chapter is to show that the argument does fail; there is nothing in posthypnotic suggestion, as Freud views it, that forces him "to insist upon the importance of the distinction between *conscious* and *unconscious*," as he claims.[2] Here is the argument as Freud states it:

> A person is put into a hypnotic state and is subsequently aroused. While he was in the hypnotic state, under the influence of the physician, he was ordered to execute a certain action at a certain fixed moment after his awakening, say half an hour later. He awakes, and seems fully conscious and in his ordinary condition; he has no recollection of his hypnotic state, and yet at the pre-arranged moment there rushes into his mind the impulse to do such and such a thing, and he does it consciously though not knowing why. It seems impossible to give any other description of the phenomenon than to say that the order had been present in the mind of the person in a condition of latency, or had been present unconsciously, until the given moment ca.ne, and then had become conscious. But not the whole of it emerged into consciousness: only the conception of the act to be executed — the order, the influence of the physician, the recollection of the hypnotic state, remained unconscious even then.

> But we have more to learn from such an experiment. We are led from the purely descriptive to a *dynamic* view of the phenomenon. The idea of the action ordered in hypnosis not only became an object of conscious-

1. See, for example, Freud, "A Note on the Unconscious in Psycho-Analysis," vol. 12; *Introductory Lectures on Psycho-Analysis*, 16:277–78; and "Some Elementary Lessons in Psycho-Analysis," vol. 23.

2. Freud, " A Note on the Unconscious in Psycho-Analysis," 12:261. Readers of Wittgenstein's *Philosophical Investigations* will easily recognize that the argument presented here derives from lines of thought to be found in what has come to be known as the Private Language Argument in that work.

ness at a certain moment, but the most striking aspect of the fact is that this idea grew *active*; it was translated into action as soon as consciousness became aware of its presence. The real stimulus to the action being the order of the physician, it is hard not to concede that the idea of the physician's order became active, too. Yet this last idea did not reveal itself to consciousness, as did its outcome, the idea of the action; it remained unconscious, and so it was *active and unconscious* at the same time.[3]

By the end of the first paragraph, the existence of unconscious ideas has been "proved," if at all, only in the trivial sense that forgotten ideas have been shown to exist, which is merely another way of saying that people sometimes forget things they were aware of earlier. Freud's claim at the end of paragraph one that

(a) the idea of the order remained unconscious

is equivalent to

(b) the subject did not remember the order.

Doubt that anything has really been proved up to that point arises from Freud's claiming both that when "the given moment came," "the order . . . had become conscious" (in the paragraph's next-to-last sentence) and also that at the same time "the order . . . remained unconscious even then" (in the last sentence of the paragraph), a curiously hypnotizing formulation for an argument of such intuitive plausibility. It is, after all, intrinsically odd to say of someone who does not remember being ordered to do a thing that, when he does it, the order became conscious.

The crux of the argument really lies in the second paragraph. For if the hypnotic subject did not perform the action ordered, but merely became conscious of the idea of the act, say, then the sense in which the idea of the order was unconscious would be merely that the order had been forgotten, and no more than that. So Freud is correct in emphasizing in paragraph two that the argument depends upon some idea — the idea of the act ordered — "becoming active." Freud sees the need to show that some idea, while remaining forgot-

3. Ibid.

ten, "becomes active." But the idea of the act does not illustrate this, since it becomes conscious, too. So Freud argues that

(c) the real stimulus to the act is the order of the physician

therefore,

(d) the idea of the physician's order became active, too.

Unless (d) can be proved, no important sense in which ideas are unconscious has been shown. Does (c) imply (d)? To see why this is doubtful, we need to examine the peculiar meanings of the expressions "real stimulus" and "becoming active," when applied to ideas. The former, it will be argued, represents Freud's commitment in this proof to an unacceptable theory of causality, especially mental causality, while the latter expression is ambiguous.

The premise that might at first seem to justify the inference from (c) to (d) becomes clear when we ask what more must be said than

(e) the real stimulus of an act must be active at the same time as the act (or contiguous with it), or must cause something else which is active at the same time as the act (or contiguous with it).

What needs to be added to (e) to justify the inference from (c) to (d) comes out when we realize that the mere time lapse between order and act is not the obstacle to the order being the real stimulus of the act, for Freud. Freud requires that the "something else" in (e) must be a resemblance of the order, as is the idea of the order. So to capture this view, it seems, we shall need

(f) the real stimulus of an act must be active at the same time as the act (or contiguous with it), or must cause something resembling the real stimulus, that is, the idea of the real stimulus, which is active at the same time as the act (or contiguous with it).

The inference from (c) to (d) would be validated by (f); but is (f) true? It is hard to see why the thing supposed to be caused by the real stimulus must resemble the real stimulus, why it must be an idea of the real stimulus, or why it must be an idea at all. Holding (f) true is like insisting that if the match flame that ignites the fuse that detonates a stick of dynamite has gone out by the time the explosion occurs, then at the time of the explosion a "ghost" flame must still really be burning invisibly in its place.

If (f) were accepted, unconscious mental activity could be proved to exist without resorting to so unusual a phenomenon as posthypnotic suggestion; Freud might more easily have pointed to the simple fact that people obey orders to prove the same thing. We command people to do certain things in the future, and in many cases, at the time indicated, they do as they were told. Must the idea of the order intervene between the giving of the order and the act obeying it? According to (f), it is necessary; people cannot simply do as they were told. However, consider the case in which the subject has long forgotten the order—for example, a third-grade penmanship teacher may have instructed the subject as a child to cross his *t*'s horizontally, not diagonally. If the adult subject acts in conformity with that order, must we say that each crossing of a *t* now, is necessarily preceded or accompanied by the idea of the teacher's order? (To answer yes is to make the mere occurrence of habit-formation sufficient to prove the existence of unconscious mental activity.) The temptation here is to think that if the idea of the order does not become active, too, then the subject will not know he is to *do* something. He will not know he is to perform the act contained in the idea of the act which also became conscious. The idea of the order, then, explains the meaning of the idea of the act; it indicates to the subject how the idea of the act is to be taken. This is the reason for the demand in (f) that the thing caused by the real stimulus must be the idea of the real stimulus.

But if we need an additional idea, the idea of the order, to tell us what to do with the idea of the act, we shall need yet another idea to tell us what to do with the idea of the order as well. Are we to obey the order, give the order, discuss the order, rescind it, disobey it? The same problem will arise with regard to whatever additional idea is supplied and so on ad infinitum. If the idea of the order is supposed to show its meaning with unmistakably clarity, so that no further idea is necessary to render its meaning determinate, why is the idea of the act by itself not capable of the same thing—that is, of determining an action with no further idea necessary to make it operative? This infinite regress argument is not intended to show that in cases of posthypnotic suggestion (or obeying orders, generally) the idea of the order does not become active, either consciously or unconsciously. Its point is only that there is no a priori necessity of the idea of the order becoming active. If Freud's argument were all that we had in support of the claim, we would have no reason at all to believe that the idea of the order becomes active, either consciously or unconsciously, in cases of posthypnotic suggestion or any other case.

It might be argued that (f) ought to be treated as an empirical claim of some plausibility, since the best available theories demand that whenever orders are obeyed posthypnotically, the idea of the order "becomes active." Yet Freud offers no empirical evidence of the truth of (f) — his argument is designed to show that the idea of the order *must* become active if the subject is to be made to perform the act ordered. To see why (f) cannot be treated as an empirical hypothesis, however, we shall have to consider the ambiguity in speaking of an idea "becoming active."

When Freud writes of the idea of the act ordered becoming active, he means the subject performs the act. But when he writes of the idea of the order becoming active, this is assumed not to mean that the subject, for example, *gives* the order; again, the subject obeys the order, since it is the idea of the order that is supposed to activate the idea of the act. Is there any difference in meaning between the two claims — that the idea of the order became active, and the idea of the act became active? Let us suppose that there is no difference in meaning between the two claims; this is plausible since their verification is the same — the subject obeys the order. With no difference in meaning, (f) would be trivially true; but then treating (f) as an empirical hypothesis would be absurd. Saying "the best available theories demand" that (c) entails (d) would be idle.

Suppose, on the other hand, that there is a difference in meaning between the idea of the order becoming active and the idea of the act becoming active. If the difference is of the sort that has already been suggested, that is, the first gives the sense in which the second is to be taken, then (f) generates an infinite regress, which I take to be a reductio ad absurdum. That is, if the reason for supposing a difference in meaning between the idea of the order becoming active and the idea of the act becoming active is that a guarantee is needed that the occurrence of the idea of the act will result in the *doing* of the act (and I can think of no other reason for supposing that difference in meaning), then whatever idea is supposed to provide such a guarantee will also stand in need of the very same sort of guarantee; and this infinite regress is a vicious regress, that is, it is a regress that cannot even get started. Hence, (f) is either trivial or leads to a vicious infinite regress.

Assuming (f) to be essential to the posthypnotic suggestion argument, we can summarize what is objectionable about it this way; in addition to the resemblance requirement it makes, there is also the simultaneity condition — that is, the requirement that an idea be active at the same time as the effect produced by it. What makes this requirement objectionable is that in the argument requiring it, the notion of an idea's activity is mysterious, as is that of the time at which an idea is supposed to be active. What, after all, is the activity of an idea, and when does it take place? Obviously, it does not take place solely when it occurs to us consciously — for then, in posthypnotic suggestion, the idea of the order does not become active at all, contrary to what Freud tells us. Must we act on it in order for the idea in question to be active? Is the idea in question active if it merely causes some other idea, even if we don't act on either? Is the idea active when it occurs to us, or only while we act on it, or just before we do? Why can't its activity cease long before its effects begin to appear? In this argument, no criterion of when an idea is active is provided or implied, so of course we have no criterion of whether an idea is active at the same time as another idea or event. Insofar as the argument for unconscious mental activity based on posthypnotic suggestion requires that we answer such questions without a criterion for answering them, that argument is unacceptable.

I should emphasize here that I am not trying to prove -that unconscious mental activity does not exist or that such activity is not present in posthypnotic suggestion. I am merely trying to show that hypothesizing such activity is not necessary for the reasons Freud's 1912 paper claims. If there is anything wrong with Freud's other argument, the one based on resistance and transference phenomena, it does not appear to be the sort of thing I have singled out for criticism in the posthypnotic suggestion argument.

Although Freud's 1912 proof seems to have come apart in our hands, the intuitive plausibility of invoking posthypnotic suggestion to establish the existence of unconscious mental activity seems undiminished, especially when Freud's 1938 version of the same argument is compared with his earlier, more elaborate account.[4] In the later version, Freud says merely, "He [the hypnotized subject] is in ignorance of his real motive. We, however, know what it is, for we were present when the suggestion was made to him which he is now carrying out, while he himself knows nothing of the fact that it is at work in him."[5] Here, "his real motive," what is at work in him, is simply "the suggestion [that] was made to him," that is, the order; with the removal of the distinctions needed to define which idea "became active" at the requisite time by virtue of its being "the real stimulus" of the act, the new version of the argument seems persuasive *to us*. That it was not necessarily so to Freud's audience earlier in the century is clear when we consider William James's elaborate objections to the concept of unconscious mental activity in chapter 6 of his *Principles of Psychology*.

JAMES'S CRITIQUE OF THE IDEA OF
UNCONSCIOUS MENTAL ACTIVITY

Of course Freud and psychoanalysis are not referred to in James's *Principles of Psychology* (first published in 1890), but James means his conclusions to rule out the unconscious entirely as "pure mythology,"[6] "one tissue of confusion,"[7] an "unintelligible and fantastical"[8] notion. Although James's criticisms are powerful and undermine several notions of unconscious processes, the possibility that the psychoanalytic concept evades his arguments needs to be

4. Freud, "Some Elementary Lessons in Psycho-Analysis," 23:285.
5. Ibid.
6. James, *Principles of Psychology*, 170.
7. Ibid., 172.
8. Ibid., 173.

considered. This may be hard to see since James believes he has destroyed the basis for any and all possible concepts of unconscious ideation, not merely the ten he examines. He writes:

> There is only one 'phase' in which an idea can be, and that is a fully conscious condition. If it is not in that condition, then it is not at all. Something else is, in its place. The something else may be a merely physical brain-process, or it may be another conscious idea. Either of these things may perform much the same *function* as the first idea, refer to the same object, and roughly stand in the same relations to the upshot of our thought. But there is no reason why we should throw away the logical principle of identity in psychology, and say that, however it may fare in the outer world, the mind at any rate is a place in which a thing can be all kinds of other things without ceasing to be itself as well.[9]

There are two arguments intertwined here; one, an a priori argument (in two parts) for the claim that no idea can be unconscious, states that to deny this is to "throw away the logical principle of identity. . . . So we seem not only to have ascertained the unintelligibility of the notion that a mental fact can be two things at once, and that what seems like one feeling, of blueness for example, or of hatred, may really and 'unconsciously' be ten thousand elementary feelings which do not resemble blueness or hatred at all, but we find that we can express all of the observed facts in other ways."[10] The second argument here claims that in all cases in which the temptation to insert an unconscious idea arises, the observed phenomena can be "expressed" instead by reference to brain processes or conscious ideas. This second argument has the look of a factual claim; yet given the a priori argument, one wonders what it would be like to find a case in which the employment of unconscious ideas was tempting, but in which conscious ideas or brain processes could not express the observed facts.

James's a priori argument seems to rest on the undefended claim that an idea can exist in only one "phase": a fully conscious condition. Perhaps this is assumed because a certain mental picture of

---

9. Ibid. Unfortunately, James provides no expansion on the subsidiary claim here that a brain process may refer to an object.

10. Ibid., 175.

what an unconscious idea would have to be — that is, something at once conscious (insofar as it is an idea at all) and also not conscious — is intuitively repugnant; thinking in this way is to "throw away the logical principle of identity in psychology." Against James it might be pointed out that arguing in this way is extremely unpragmatic — what mental picture, after all, goes with our everyday talk of people being only half-awake or half-asleep? The notion that James treats as an axiom, "an idea can only exist in a fully conscious condition," seems no more pragmatic than are the useless notions of the unconscious he rightly opposes. James writes as if he had a complete list (and knows it to be complete) of possible senses of the concept. However, I shall try to show that James fails to consider the sense of the concept employed in psychoanalysis.

If we turn to the second part of what I have labeled James's a priori argument, James seems to treat the ten arguments for unconscious mental activity that he considers as variants of one inference — all try to show that some mental fact is really more complex than it seems to the person in whose mind it exists, that is, that its parts are unconscious "elementary feelings" differing qualitatively from it. James seems to think that arguing in this way is also to "throw away the logical principle of identity" but in a less obvious way than the first part of the a priori argument claims. Yet there is not any apparent contradiction, for example, in saying that something blue is composed of parts, many or all of which are not themselves blue. Indeed, to suppose that the "elementary feelings" must all resemble the feeling they are parts of would be to commit the fallacy of division (predicating of each member of a collective what is true only of the collective), a fallacy James himself rightly finds in the first argument for unconscious mental states that he considers. According to that argument, "The *minimum visibile,* the *minimum audibile,* are objects composed of parts. How can the whole affect the sense unless each part does? And yet each part does so without being separately sensible."[11] James quotes Leibniz, who argues as follows:

> I am accustomed to use the example of the roaring of the sea with which one is assailed when near the shore. To hear this noise as one does, one

11. Ibid., 164.

must hear the parts which compose its totality, that is, the noise of each wave . . . although this noise would not be noticed if its wave were alone. One must be affected a little by the movement of one wave, one must have perception of each several noise, however small it be. Otherwise one would not hear that of 100,000 waves, for of 100,000 zeros one can never make a quantity.[12]

To this, James properly replies that "each infra-sensible stimulus to a nerve no doubt affects the nerve and helps the birth of sensation when the other stimuli come. But this affection is a nerve-affection, and there is not the slightest ground for supposing it to be a 'perception' unconscious of itself."[13]

Arguments such as the one James replies to here suppose that "mental states are composite in structure, made up of smaller states combined," which he labeled the "Mind-Stuff Theory."[14] Against this theory, James asserts that "there *are* no unperceived units of mind-stuff preceding and composing the full consciousness. The latter is itself an immediate psychic fact and bears an immediate relation to the neural state which is its unconditional accompaniment."[15] One argument in support of this claim is that "We cannot mix feelings as such, though we may mix the objects we feel, and from *their* mixtures get new feelings."[16] Another reason is that feelings cannot mix themselves: "*All the 'combinations' which we actually know are* EFFECTS, *wrought by the units said to be 'combined,'* UPON SOME ENTITY OTHER THAN THEMSELVES . . . the compounded idea is an altogether new psychic fact to which the separate ideas stand in the relation not of constituents, but of occasions of production."[17]

Strictly, then, James's own arguments against the mind-stuff theory do not imply the absurdity of any and all theories of unconscious mental states; only those theories that analyze conscious states by

12. Ibid.
13. Ibid., 165.
14. Ibid., 145.
15. Ibid., 157.
16. Ibid.
17. Ibid., 158–61. Emphasis in original.

"decomposition" are objectionable,that is, analyses claiming that conscious mental states necessarily have unconscious mental "constituents." Such theories instantiate the mind-stuff theory; but theories claiming that conscious mental states have other *conscious* mental states as constituents instantiate the mind-stuff theory, too, and James emphatically rejects them.[18] By contrast, James endorses analyses that invoke conscious mental states as "occasions of production" of other conscious states, so he ought to find no objection in comparable analyses invoking unconscious mental states for the same purpose.[19] In short, it is not the doctrine of unconscious mental states in itself that is the proper target of James's criticism; rather, it is one sort of analysis resulting in that doctrine that is. When any analysis of mental states assumes that conscious mental states have constituent mental states, conscious or unconscious, James's criticism of the mind-stuff theory authorizes him to reject that analysis but gives no reason to reject other analyses that assume that conscious mental states have conscious or unconscious "occasions of production." In the *Principles,* James does not seem to have considered the possibility that the two views, the mind-stuff theory and the idea of unconscious mental states, are separable, that one might be asserted without commitment to the other. James simply assumed that rejection of the mind-stuff theory required rejection as well of any and all theories of unconscious mental states. A parallel between James and Wittgenstein can be seen here; both mistakenly assume that ideas of unconscious mental activity always rest on the same erroneous view of mental states, the mind-stuff theory in James corresponding to what I called the I-statement or genetic fallacy model in Wittgenstein. In the *Principles,* James, unlike Wittgenstein, had no psychoanalytic examples to grapple with, and so he simply assumed that the sort of criticism that dispatches Leibniz's "roaring of

18. In his objections to the tenth proof, James rejects claims that some conscious mental states are constituents of other conscious states (ibid., 172–75).

19. For example, instead of unconscious mental states as explanation of our acquired (intelligent) habitual actions, James proposes "perceptions . . . performed consciously, only so quickly and inattentively that no *memory* of them remains" (165).

the sea" example will also take care of all the other hypothetical cases of unconscious mental states, too. However, by the time he reached his own last case, the loving feelings case in the tenth proof, he seems to have experienced doubts on this point, as we shall see.

The a priori part of James's criticism does not follow from any of the points he makes against particular arguments in support of unconscious mental processes. Of these, the fifth proof is of interest because that proof is a little like Freud's 1912 proof, and the seventh proof seems to be a reincarnation of Plato's recollection argument in the *Meno* and *Phaedo*. In reply to the first five proofs James places somewhat more emphasis on the claim that phenomena that seem to require unconscious ideas are more plausibly explained by conscious ideas that are unattended to, quickly gone, forgotten.[20] In reply to proofs six through nine, James argues that nerve-affections or brain processes, not unconscious ideas, explain the problematic phenomena. Here is the fifth proof:

> In trance, artificial or pathological, long and complex performances, involving the use of the reasoning powers, are executed, of which the patient is wholly unaware on coming to. *Reply.* Rapid and complete obliviscence is certainly the explanation here. The analogue again is hypnotism. Tell the subject of an hypnotic trance, during his trance, that he *will* remember, and he may remember everything perfectly when he awakes, though without your telling him no memory would have remained. The extremely rapid obliviscence of common dreams is a familiar fact.[21]

The argument for unconscious mental states here does not depend on the phenomenon of posthypnotic suggestion, as in Freud; it is posthypnotic forgetting that is supposed to need explanation. People come out of trances, during which their reasoning powers are employed, and recall nothing of what they did during the trance. The implication is that if they had been consciously performing in trance, they would remember something of it on coming out of the trance. Since nothing is recalled, they must have been unconsciously reasoning, performing.

Posthypnotic suggestion occurs in the Reply to this argument and

20. Ibid., 165.
21. Ibid., 166.

causes no puzzlement for James; he is not tempted by the thought that if, when awake, people do what they were ordered to do during the trance (here, to remember), then there must be an unconscious idea causing them to do so. Rather, the fact that people can be made to remember what went on in the trance proves that they must have had conscious ideas during the trance. Although he does not say so here, for James, such conscious ideas during trance are actually states of a "secondary self," "a split-off, limited and buried, but yet a fully conscious self,"[22] about which he is surprisingly reticent in his discussion of the ten proofs.[23] James emphasizes that the two selves "mutually ignore each other,"[24] which seems hard to reconcile with his claim, quoted above, that if you tell the subject of a hypnotic trance, during the trance, that posthypnotically he *will* remember, he will. For the self which then remembers must be the primary self, yet the order was given to the secondary self, in which case the two selves appear to communicate with each other.

That Freud's posthypnotic suggestion argument presents no difficulty for James is also apparent in his treatment of the fourth proof:

> *Fourth Proof.* Problems unsolved when we go to bed are found solved in the morning when we awake. Somnambulists do rational things. We awaken punctually at an hour predetermined overnight, etc. Unconscious thinking, volition, time-registration, etc., must have presided over these acts.
>
> *Reply.* Consciousness forgotten, as in the hypnotic trance.[25]

Here, the sleeper awakens at a predetermined hour consciously intending to do so; that conscious intention is quickly forgotten. Sim-

22. Ibid., 209. James also uses posthypnotic suggestion to illustrate the activity of a "sub-conscious . . . secondary personage" (206–7).

23. The idea of "a split-off condition of portions of consciousness" surfaces at only one point in James's examination of the ten proofs for unconscious mental activity — that is, in his reply to the second proof (165). The reference there to material in chapter 10 might relate especially to automatic writing phenomena, discussed on pages 398–400. James regarded such phenomena as "the most striking and cogent" proof of a secondary consciousness's existence (204).

24. Ibid., 206; see also 208.

25. Ibid., 166.

ilarly, presumably, the hypnotic trance subject performs, as ordered, under the influence of a conscious idea, which is also quickly forgotten (perhaps later to be recalled, along with everything else). Here, as elsewhere, James leaves unexplained what in any particular case justifies favoring explanation by conscious ideas rather than by brain-tracts, or vice versa. Indeed, once the idea of a second consciousness is introduced, it is striking that James is silent about why some phenomena call for explanation in terms of forgotten conscious states *simpliciter,* as opposed to those needing explanation in terms of conscious states of a second consciousness. So the resort to quickly forgotten conscious ideas seems doubly arbitrary here. Besides, how quickly would an idea have to be forgotten for James to begin to consider the possibility of its being an unconscious idea, not a conscious one? Given James's a priori argument, the answer must be that the idea remains a conscious one no matter how quickly it is forgotten. But then can an idea be forgotten instantaneously? If not, why not? If so, "instantaneously forgotten conscious idea" would seem to be a characterization hard to distinguish from "unconscious idea."

These remarks are not meant to prove that unconscious ideas *must* be invoked if posthypnotic suggestion is to be explained. They are meant merely to undermine the refusal to invoke them under any circumstances. James is committed to the view that unconscious ideas must *not* be invoked under any circumstances, since the very notion of an unconscious idea is unintelligible. Given his firm commitment to that claim, we cannot ascribe to James a version of his a posteriori argument which treats it merely as an application of some principle of parsimony — a version of it claiming merely that we ought to stay with explanations involving entities known to exist (that is, brain processes and conscious ideas) as long as possible, before postulating new entities, such as unconscious ideas. Since unconscious ideas are unintelligible, James holds that they may not be appealed to in any circumstances. So James's a posteriori argument must also be taken as stating a necessary truth — that conscious ideas or brain processes can explain all mental phenomena. The *can* in this claim expresses logical possibility, not any pragmatic potentiality present in superior degree in explanations restricted to brain processes and conscious ideas over explanations involving other sorts of entities.

IS UNCONSCIOUS MENTAL ACTIVITY EVER NECESSARY?

Whereas Freud painted himself into a corner trying to prove the necessity of a concept — *unconscious mental activity* — in order for a certain phenomenon — post-hypnotic suggestion — to be possible, James has done the same thing trying to prove the nonnecessity (indeed, the absurdity) of the same concept. Such discussions, are probably doomed to failure and are comparable in difficulty to the task of trying to prove the necessity (or absurdity) of the concept of *material body,* for example, in explaining our sense perceptions. The obstacle to success in such proofs may lie not so much in the inherent difficulty of the project in any particular case as in the absence of any prior understanding about what doing such a thing consists in. What quite generally should we call *proving the necessity of a concept* (or proving its nonnecessity) *in explaining a phenomenon?* Do we have any uncontroversial examples of such a proof? It seems we lack criteria for success in proofs of that sort.

If we turn instead to the more manageable question, are there any scientific advantages to adopting the concept of unconscious mental activity, reasons can be given for doing so, as James himself may have begun to suspect; even in the *Principles,* by the time he came to the last of his attempted refutations of the idea, there are indications that his certainty about the correctness of his position was already beginning to waver. Thus, the last proof considered, the tenth, which deals with a case close to Freud's resistance cases, receives the longest and most elaborate critical response from James. But unlike the other nine, he begins his response to the tenth proof under the more tentative heading, Objection, instead of Reply, which is his label in all the other cases. In addition, the tenth proof begins after a space separating it from the end of the reply to the ninth proof, another difference in format that sets this proof and reply off from the others. Responding to the tenth proof forces James to introduce more elaborate principles than the assertion that nerve affections, brain processes or quickly forgotten conscious states can explain the problem cases as well as unconscious mental activity can. Lastly, the tenth proof introduces cases of a different sort from those considered in the preceding nine — the tenth proof concerns cases in which introspection alone seems to determine what unconscious ideas a person is supposed to have had. In the preceding nine proofs, as in Freud's post hypnotic suggestion argument, whatever unconscious ideas are supposed to be at work can be derived from the subject's behavior; in Freud's argument, it could not turn out to be any other idea than that of the order. Certainly nothing the subject of hypnosis might have to say, for example, his free associations, has any authority to show otherwise. According to James's tenth proof,

> there is a great class of experiences in our mental life which may be described as discoveries that a subjective condition which we have been having is really something different from what we had supposed. We suddenly find ourselves bored by a thing which we thought we were enjoying well enough; or in love with a person whom we imagined we only liked. Or else we deliberately analyze our motives, and find that at bottom they contain jealousies and cupidities which we little expected to be there. Our feelings towards people are perfect wells of motivation, unconscious of itself, which introspection brings to light. And our sensations likewise: we constantly discover new elements in sensations which we have been in the habit of receiving all our days, elements, too, which have been there from the first, since otherwise we should have been unable to distinguish the sensations containing them from others nearly allied. The elements must exist for we use them to discriminate by; but they must exist in an unconscious state, since we so completely fail to single them out.[26]

It would be easy to think of Freud as engaged in a "deliberate analysis of motives," and to suppose that if James does successfully attack this sort of program, then Freud's program is defeated as well. James writes:

> When I decide that I have, without knowing it, been for several weeks in love, I am simply giving a name to a state which previously *I have not*

26. Ibid., 170–71.

named, but which was fully conscious; which had no residual mode of being except the manner in which it was conscious; and which, though it was a feeling towards the same person for whom I now have a much more inflamed feeling, and though it continuously led into the latter, and is similar enough to be called by the same name, is yet in no sense identical with the latter, and least of all in an "unconscious" way.[27]

James confuses the issue here by assuming that by the time the feeling is named, the feeling has become more inflamed; presumably, cases are possible in which the feeling's intensity is unchanged, and all that changes is its being named. Then the question is, does merely naming the feeling make it a different feeling? James's answer is that it does. To see how extreme James's position is, consider that even if it were conceded that when we name the feeling, we are in a different psychic state from the one we were in when we had not yet named it, James will not be satisfied; he requires that the two states must also involve different *feelings.* The problem is clearer in his earlier discussion (two pages before) of arguments for unconscious mental processes based on "sensations and the new features in them which attention brings to light."[28] According to one such argument,

> we all know *practically* the difference between the so-called sonant and the so-called surd consonants, between D, B, Z, G, V, and T, P, S, K, F, respectively. But comparatively few persons know the difference *theoretically,* until their attention has been called to what it is, when they perceive it readily enough. The sonants are nothing but the surds plus a certain element, which is alike in all, superadded. That element is the laryngeal sound with which they are uttered, surds having no such accompaniment. When we hear the sonant letter, both its component elements must really be in our mind; but we remain unconscious of what they really are, and mistake the letter for a simple quality of sound until an effort of attention teaches us its two components.[29]

James's objection to this argument is that

> the sensations of the B and the V when we attend to these sounds and analyze out the laryngeal contribution which makes them differ from P

27. Ibid., 174.
28. Ibid., 172.
29. Ibid., 171.

and F respectively, are *different sensations* from those of the B and the V taken in a simple way. They stand, it is true, for the *same letters,* and thus mean the *same outer realities;* but they are different mental affections, and certainly depend on widely different processes of cerebral activity. It is unbelievable that two mental states so different as the passive reception of a sound as a whole, and the analysis of that whole into distinct ingredients by voluntary attention, should be due to processes at all similar.[30]

Without any argument, James slides here from

(a) having a sensation in a simple way and analytically attending to what produced it (while having it) are two different mental states

to

(b) the sensations in the two states are different sensations.

Whereas (a) seems to be a truism, (b) does not.[31] Clearly, James feels compelled to assert (b) by his rejection of the mind-stuff theory; to deny (b) seems to imply the sensation had in a simple way is also a constituent of the analytical attention. Even if we assume his rejection of that theory is correct, it is odd that James does not consider that there might be senses of "same" and "constituent" in regard to sensations such that the sensation can be said to be the same in the two mental states without that implying the sensation is a constituent of either. After all, sensations are not like coffee cups; we have no criteria to distinguish numerical identity as opposed to exact similarity in the former, as we do in the latter. To find (b) doubtful, one need not commit oneself categorically to

30. Ibid., 172–73.
31. Ibid., 185–87. By this point, James treats the difference between *mental state* and *feeling* as a question of nomenclature. And he decides to ignore the difference and to treat them as equivalent, using *thought* or *feeling* "according to the convenience of the context" (186). However, his reason for doing so seems to rest on the need for "a general term by which to designate all states of consciousness merely as such, and apart from their particular quality or cognitive function" (185). Adherence to James's decision would eliminate the difference between (a) and (b); yet the lack of a more compelling argument apparently leaves us free to refrain from following suit. Considering how much hinges on it in the earlier discussion of unconscious mental states, it seems odd to treat the matter as nothing more than a question of nomenclature.

(c) in the two mental states, the sensations are the same,

though ordinary speech permits it.

In his other case, in which "I decide that I have, without knowing it, been for several weeks in love," James obscures the comparable transition from (a) to (b) by underdescribing it. Thus, he does not tell us whether the decision or realization in that case was gradual, sudden, or surprising; such vagueness obscures the transformation of the case from one in which it is my realization about my feelings that is new to me, to one in which I am simply having new feelings. But is my surprise at (i) having new feelings the same thing as my surprise at both (ii) realizing what feelings I have been having, along with (iii) not having realized before what I have been feeling? James implies (ii) and (iii) are the same thing as (i). The case started out to mark a contrast, which has evaporated by the time James has finished with it. Saying

(d) I have been in love for several weeks without knowing it

seems to conflict with his claim that, in saying I have been in love for several weeks,

(e) I am simply giving a name to a state which previously *I have not named.*

For (e) implies that I have merely refrained from naming some feeling, one which I could have, would have, named had the question arisen. After all, I am not now naming the numerous things within my visual field, but I could name them if necessary. It would be absurd to say that I have been seeing them *without knowing it* merely because I have continually refrained from naming them. But (d) is not always consistent with these implications, since, at least in some cases, it might not be true that up to now I could have, would have, named my feeling had the question arisen.

It does not help efforts to render James's point that (e) in itself blurs the difference between *giving* a name *to* a feeling and merely naming the feeling, that is, giving the name *of* the feeling. Concerning the former, it seems doubtful whether we ever do that with regard to feelings at all, reserving it instead for newborns, creations such as novels, poems, plays, and so on, where *choice* exists in what we name the thing; concerning the latter, even considerable uncertainty about how the feeling should be named is different from choosing a name for it. When is it appropriate to speak of choosing a name for a feeling? Whatever contexts we imagine seem far from James's case.

Furthermore, James concedes, perhaps unwittingly, that the "fully conscious" loving feeling did have a "residual mode of being," after all, namely, "the manner in which it was conscious" that is, *named or unnamed*).[32] If the scope of (d) includes cases in which I could not, would not, have named my feeling had the question arisen before, it seems strange to narrow the focus of the discussion about whether unconscious mental states exist to such things as the loving feeling; rather, the focus should be on the manner in which the feeling is conscious, that is, named or unnamed — where unnamed can mean *unable to be named*. In that discussion, why is not the failure or inability to name one's own feeling as interesting as the feeling itself? Could the feeling have been "fully conscious" if at the same time I could not have named it? Even if we grant that the feeling was then fully conscious, why was I unable to name it until now? Why didn't I, or couldn't I, name my feeling before now? What produced my inattention in the first case, what prevented me from being able to attend in the second?

Can the answer to these last questions lie merely in the faintness of the feeling until now, as James seems to suppose? Such an explana-

---

32. It is unclear whether saying this is consistent with James's earlier claim (ibid., 173) concerning the psychic states involved when the B is taken in a simple way and when the sound is attended to analytically, that "Each of them [the psychic states] is a conscious fact; none of them has any mode of being whatever except a certain way of being felt at the moment of being present." For "(i) the manner in which the feeling was conscious" seems to mean the same as "(ii) the psychic state's way of being felt at the moment of being conscious"; but concerning (i), James says it is a residual mode of being, the only one the feeling has, over and above being fully conscious, whereas concerning (ii) he seems to say that over and above being conscious, the psychic state has no residual mode of being. The confusion is assisted, as before, by the blurring (in the quote from 173) of *psychic states* and feelings.

tion ought to give us pause; after all, faint feelings can normally be named in the present, even if they dwindle, rather than grow more inflamed. The suspicion that James is unable to explain my past failure or inability to name the feeling is reinforced when he writes:

> A faint feeling may be looked back upon and classified and understood in its relations to what went before or after it in the stream of thought. But it, on the one hand, and the later state of mind which knows all these things about it, on the other, are surely not two conditions, one conscious and the other "unconscious," of the same identical psychic fact. . . . The only identity to be found among our successive ideas is their similarity of cognitive or representative function as dealing with the same objects.[33]

For James, it appears to be the mere *faintness* of the feeling that explains my inability to name it before now. It is hard to see how this can be right, however; for if the feeling was until now so faint that I was incapable of naming it, how can I now claim to be able to see its previous *similarity* (and continuity) with my present nameable feeling?[34] How can I claim to know that the earlier and later feelings are "similar enough to be called by the same name"[35] if, until now, I could not have named the earlier one because of its faintness? Whatever features in the earlier feeling are supposed to have made it similar enough to call it by the same name as the later feeling are features which, if I had been able to notice them, would have enabled me to name the feeling before now. But that I was unable to do. In the end, it is hard to see how to reconcile James's three claims concerning the feeling in question —

I felt love without knowing it until now.
That loving feeling was too faint to notice.
My present feeling is similar to that earlier, faint one.

In different ways, any two of these statements seem to conflict with the third. Thus, asserting the first and second creates the puzzle of how I can know the third to be true; claiming the second and third casts doubt on the truth of the first; and asserting the first and third

33. Ibid., 174–75.
34. Ibid., 174.
35. Ibid.

raises doubts about the truth of the second. The point is not that there is something problematic about saying of my own past feeling that I was unaware of it until now, that it was a faint feeling, and that it was similar to my present one. Rather, the problem lies in claiming both that the feeling's faintness *explains* my previous lack of awareness of it, yet also that it was similar to my present feeling.

It is remarkable that James does not find more difficulty than he does in saying that the later, nameable loving feeling is *similar* to the earlier, faint (and therefore unnamed or unnameable) feeling; for he explicitly denies any similarity at all in a comparable case on the preceding page: "The man who learns for the first time how the closure of his glottis feels, experiences in this discovery an absolutely new psychic modification, the like of which he never had before. He had another feeling before, a feeling incessantly renewed, and of which the same glottis was the organic starting point; but that was not the later feeling in an 'unconscious' state; it was a feeling *sui generis* altogether, although it took cognizance of the same bodily part, the glottis."[36] Presumably in one case, the subject knew what loving feelings felt like before experiencing the faint feelings he now knows he felt, whereas here, the subject "learns for the first time how the closure of his glottis feels." But it is hard to see why that should be a relevant difference; after all, before first learning how the closure of his glottis feels, the man in question had feelings that "took cognizance of the same bodily part." Why is that "similarity of cognitive or representative function as dealing with the same objects" (which, for James is "[t]he only identity to be found among our successive ideas") not enough to make these earlier and later feelings "similar enough to be called by the same name," as James asserts of the earlier and later loving feelings?[37] Even if not similar enough to be named the same, the earlier and later glottal feelings are similar — so it cannot be said of the later feeling that it was "an absolutely new psychic modification, the like of which he never had before."[38] James's judgments of similarity and difference with regard to feel-

36. Ibid., 173.
37. Ibid., 174–75.
38. Ibid., 173.

ings and mental states generally have an arbitrariness about them that undermines the arguments in which they figure.

Three interim conclusions can be stated about James's treatment of the unconscious mental activity hypothesis; first, despite his rhetoric, James has no good argument for completely rejecting the hypothesis — at best, he has an argument for rejecting one version of it, that is, the one according to which certain conscious mental states have unconscious mental states as *constituents.* It remains to be seen whether it is that version of the hypothesis that Freud's central examples, for example, in the 1915 paper "The Unconscious" rest on. Second, James's account of posthypnotic suggestion is flawed; he tries to treat that phenomenon as one easily explained by conscious ideas — but by his own account elsewhere in the *Principles,* the conscious ideas required are ideas in a second consciousness, which James fails to mention in his attempted refutation of the posthypnotic suggestion argument. James seems to be trying to evade acknowledging that extraordinary means are needed to explain posthypnotic suggestion — for, of course, invoking a second consciousness is hardly less drastic a measure than invoking unconscious mental activity. Besides, James's account seems incoherent, since he claims primary and secondary selves "mutually ignore each other," yet in posthypnotic suggestion the two selves apparently must communicate with each other. Third, the loving feelings case in James's tenth proof is one for which James has no plausible explanation apart from some version of the unconscious mental activity hypothesis; James's proposed alternative account bristles with inconsistencies and raises more questions than it can answer.

The price to be paid for not invoking unconscious mental activity as an explanatory concept increases even more if we turn to the sort of cases that James does not even think about, that is, cases such as the ones Freud lists at the start of his 1915 paper, "The Unconscious" — parapraxes, dreams, symptoms.[39] In each, as most clearly in the case of dreams, it commonly happens that a mental state seems to mean something to the person whose mental state it is, even

---

39. Freud, "The Unconscious," 14:66. The absence of the entire subject of dreams from James's *Principles* is remarkable.

though that person does not know what it means.[40] The dream seems to its dreamer to mean something; what can we say about that apparent meaning without recourse to unconscious mental activity? In the posthypnotic suggestion case, I have argued, we could say that the order caused the subject to obey without our having to say that the *idea* of the order was "active" at the time the awakened subject obeyed. Might we then say that the dream's meaning (that is, the "'dream-thought" combined with the "dream-work," according to Freud) *caused* the dream to occur but need not be assumed to be operative at the time the dreamer wonders about the dream's meaning?[41] Might the meaning of the dream be merely whatever caused it to be dreamt, and nothing more in the present? The trouble is that saying this seems to imply that the dream meant something in the past, but no longer has any meaning. After all, it is in the present that the dream-work, say, still prevents us from awareness of the dream-thought. If the dream-thought and dream-work had merely occurred in the past and were not still occurring, either the dream would now seem to have no meaning or its meaning would be evident to the dreamer. But neither is the case. The mental state of a dreamer wondering what a dream means seems to cry out for explanation in terms of unconscious mental activity. As long as dreams seem to dreamers to have meanings that they do not yet think they understand, it is hard to see how the sort of thing Freud says about such mental states can be entirely avoided — that in them, unconscious mental processes produced the dream in the first place and continue to prevent the dreamer from knowing the dream's meaning.

The contrast with the posthypnotic suggestion case is striking, especially in Freud's final presentation of that case:

> Here is more or less what happens. The doctor enters the hospital ward, puts his umbrella in the corner, hypnotizes one of the patients and says to him: "I'm going out now. When I come in again, you will come to meet me

40. Freud says something similar about jokes as well (*Jokes and Their Relation to the Unconscious*, 8:102, 132, 154).

41. James might concede that the dream-thought and dream-work produce dreams, especially if they are seen as conscious states that are quickly gone and unattended to.

with my umbrella open and hold it over my head." The doctor and his assistants then leave the ward. As soon as they come back, the patient, who is no longer under hypnosis, carries out exactly the instructions that that were given him while he was hypnotized. The doctor questions him: "What's this you're doing? What's the meaning of all this?" The patient is clearly embarrassed. He makes some lame remark such as "I only thought, doctor, as it's raining outside you'd open your umbrella in the room before you went out." The explanation is obviously quite inadequate and made up on the spur of the moment to offer some sort of motive for his senseless behaviour. It is clear to us spectators that he is in ignorance of his real motive.[42]

Here Freud emphasizes how meaningless the act performed is for the patient. By contrast, dreamers treat their dreams as meaningful, although they are as ignorant of what their meanings might be as this patient was. So there is a second question the hypothesis of unconscious mental activity seems suited to answer: namely, why do we treat some objectively meaningless things — dreams, parapraxes, symptoms (and jokes, too) — as meaningful, but not others? Why do posthypnotic subjects' impulses and actions seem meaningless to them but their dreams, for example, do not? It is hard to see how to answer such questions without resorting to unconscious mental activity, or something very like it.

If resistance phenomena are central to the psychoanalytic account of unconscious mental activity, it remains to be seen what mental states can be resisted; that is, what account shall we give of the unconscious mental activity that both provides the meaning of the dream and explains the resistances encountered in seeking its meaning? The search for an answer to this question is, in part, the subject of chapter 3.

42. Freud, "Some Elementary Lessons in Psycho-Analysis," 23:285.

3

. . . .

The Problem of Unverifiability

An important objection to Freud, about which I have said little so far, might be put this way: the unconscious and the transformations of impulse supposed to take place in it, especially repression, are unobservable. By itself, this is not a defect in a theory claiming to be scientific. However, as Ernest Nagel writes, it is a defect if none of the unobservables can be "*tied down* to *fairly definite* and unambiguously specified observable materials, by way of rules of procedure, variously called 'correspondence rules,' 'coordinating definitions,' and 'operational definitions.' "[1] Can the unconscious mental processes Freud refers to be tied down in the way required? Even if they can, it must also be possible "to deduce determinate consequences from the assumptions of theory, so that we can decide on the basis of logical considerations, and prior to the examination of any empirical data, whether or not an alleged consequence of the theory is indeed implied by the latter. For unless this requirement is fulfilled, the theory has no definite content, and questions as to what the theory asserts cannot be settled except by recourse to some privileged authority or arbitrary caprice."[2] J. O.

1. Nagel, "Methodological Issues in Psychoanalytic Theory," 40.
2. Ibid., 39–40.

Wisdom and Peter Madison think psychoanalysis does (or can be made to) conform to the model of scientific theory sketched by Nagel.[3] Gardner Lindzey, Ernest Nagel, and Alasdair MacIntyre think it fails.[4] I shall first examine MacIntyre's argument in *The Unconscious* and then consider some features of his model that may allow us to challenge its appropriateness.

According to MacIntyre, the skeleton of Freud's theoretical structure is exhibited in the following three claims:

1. [There is] a correlation between certain types of childhood experience and certain types of adult behaviour.
2. . . . remembering childhood situations (and abreacting or achieving catharsis in some other way of the emotions connected with them) will alter behaviour.
3. . . . the reason why childhood events are correlated with adult experience *and* why their recall to memory has therapeutic power is *because* memories have been repressed, have been operative in some form or other in the unconscious and have manifested themselves in overt behaviour.[5]

MacIntyre writes that (1) and (2) omit much that Freud would consider essential in his theoretical account — "Freud pins everything" on (3). I shall concentrate on (3) and the problems it raises; MacIntyre clearly believes that (1) and (2) offer no particular difficulties — they are observably true or false and contain no reference to unobservable entities or processes. (Of (1) he remarks that there is nothing peculiarly "Freudian" about such statements.)[6] But (3) is different, with its reference to repression and the unconscious in which memories have been operative while forgotten. For repression is an unobservable process, according to MacIntyre:

> Can we observe repression occurring in ourselves or others? Freud's terminology is obscure to me here, but at least it is quite clear, that if we

3. Wisdom, "Psycho-analytic Technology" and "Testing a Psycho-analytic Interpretation"; Madison, *Freud's Concept of Repression and Defense.*
    4. Lindzey, "Assessment of Human Motives"; Nagel, "Methodological Issues in Psychoanalytic Theory; MacIntyre, *The Unconscious.*
    5. MacIntyre, *The Unconscious,* 67–69.
    6. Ibid., 67 and 71–72.

could say "Here is an idea of an emotionally powerful kind being repressed in me" repression could not in fact occur. We must, so it would seem, be unaware of (whether we can say "unconscious of" I do not venture to say) repression occurring. Repression will therefore be unobservable. We can only infer that an idea has been repressed from subsequent behaviour and feelings.[7]

The following passage, however, specifies the correspondence rule MacIntyre would apply to verify the claim that a subject has repressed a memory: "A man may manifest great strain or anxiety and when he finds himself able to recall a particular memory, strain and anxiety vanish. To say that he repressed the memory is both to say that he was unable to recall it and that this inability is correlated with strain and anxiety. But if we used 'repression' thus we should merely be describing the phenomena which in Freud's use of the word the term is invoked in order to explain."[8] Clearly, MacIntyre thinks repression satisfies the first of the requirements for a theoretical term quoted from Nagel — in MacIntyre's terms, repression has descriptive force. MacIntyre's criticism concerns the second requirement — the need to know what results are implied by saying an idea is repressed according to psychoanalysis. In MacIntyre's terms, it is the explanatory role of the term *repression* that is problematic. He thinks the same problem arises concerning the unconscious — there is no problem in giving coordinating definitions for descriptions of behavior as "unconsciously motivated"; indeed, there is nothing peculiarly psychoanalytic or new in such descriptions. Thus, of a man who behaves in a way others take to be ambitious, MacIntyre writes:

> If Smith denied his ambition, the onus would be on him to provide us with a plausible alternative explanation of his behaviour. If he could do this, we should have to revise our verdict. If he could not, we should have a case of unconscious ambition in the ordinary pre-Freudian sense of "unconscious." If on pointing this out in suitable ways to Smith, we discover an inability in Smith to recognize his own ambition, we should have a case of unconscious ambition in something more like the Freudian sense of "unconscious." (For the purpose of illustration it does not matter that "unconscious" for the Freudian would qualify not something like "ambi-

7. Ibid., 70.
8. Ibid., 70–71.

tion" but something like "fear of his father.") And if Smith's denial of his trait was especially vehement we should perhaps treat this as almost as conclusive as an avowal.[9]

For MacIntyre, the trouble with the unconscious as a theoretical term comes in finding "determinate consequences" — explanatory force justifying the assumption of the existence of the unconscious — that is, when he seeks to satisfy

> demands that we inquire what precise explanatory role the concept of the unconscious plays. And here I find myself at a loss. For while Freud illuminatingly describes a good deal of behaviour as unconsciously motivated, and describes too how the recall of events and situations of which we had become unconscious may have a therapeutic role, he wishes to justify not just the adverb or the adjective, but also the substantive form: the unconscious. Yet from the supposition of such an entity what consequences flow that could not otherwise be predicted? Freud's hypotheses as to the infantile origin of adult traits and disorders can all be formulated without reference to it.[10]

MacIntyre does not merely mean that Freud's hypothesis of the unconscious has consequences that can be formulated in alternative non-Freudian theories that will predict the same results as Freud's and thus have the same explanatory force. MacIntyre's criticism is more drastic than this; he believes that all that Freud's theory "explains" is explainable — that is, predictable — without any alternative theory at all.

> Freud argues that a thrifty, somewhat ill-tempered attitude is the result in early life of the wrong sort of potting training or that adult attitudes to one's wife are in some cases correlated with childhood attitudes to one's mother. Bowlby argues that if at a certain period in early childhood a child is deprived of an adequate maternal figure it will later prove incapable of normal affection and will display delinquent traits. Correlations, real or alleged, of this kind might be multiplied indefinitely, and their being put forward is dependent on no particular background of theory. To test them is simply a matter of amassing evidence and as we have more

9. Ibid., 58–59.
10. Ibid., 71–72.

and more reliable records of childhood upbringing for adult patients and others, so these claims will be conclusively verified or falsified and in many cases perhaps radically modified.[11]

So, for MacIntyre, Freud's theories have no real explanatory force at all. "My thesis then is that in so far as Freud uses the concept of the unconscious as an explanatory concept, he fails, if not to justify it, at least to make clear its justification. He gives us causal explanations, certainly; but these can and apparently must stand or fall on their own feet without reference to it. He has a legitimate concept of unconscious mental activity, certainly; but this he uses to describe behaviour, not to explain it."[12] When MacIntyre writes here that the causal explanations the hypothesis of the unconscious yields can stand on their own feet without reference to it, he means that statements of the sort generalized in (1) and (2) above exhaust the sense of the predictions Freud makes, and these statements express mere correlations (between childhood experience and adult behavior, and between recall and alteration of behavior) and do not refer to repression or the unconscious at all. MacIntyre's point might be put by saying that for him, the terms *repression* and *the unconscious* as used by Freud can be given eliminative definitions that allow these terms to be replaced with references to observables in all cases. For MacIntyre, Freud's theory, stripped of its scientifically irrelevant talk of the unconscious as "an inaccessible realm of inaccessible entities existing in its own right,"[13] merely summarizes uncontroversial correlations. Hence, he concludes: "Freud's indispensable terms are 'unconscious' and 'repression' used descriptively; except in so far as illuminating description may count as a kind of explanation, their place as explanatory terms is highly dubious."[14] Summarized below are the main points in MacIntyre's criticism of (3) that I mean to examine:

a. Repression is unobservable.

11. Ibid., 67–68.
12. Ibid., 72.
13. Ibid., 71.
14 Ibid., 79.

b. To say a man has repressed a memory is to say that he is unable to recall it and that he experiences strain and anxiety correlated with this inability.

c. The unconscious is unobservable.

d. To say a man is unconsciously ambitious is to say that (i) he behaves in ways that seem ambitious to others, (ii) he cannot plausibly explain his ambitious-seeming behavior otherwise, (iii) he cannot recognize his own ambition when it is pointed out to him, and (iv) his vehement denial of his ambition is almost as conclusive as an avowal.

e. Childhood events are correlated with adult experience because memories have been repressed, have been operative in some form or other in the unconscious. 'Repression' and 'the unconscious' are introduced in order to explain such correlations.

First, I shall examine the correctness of his account of the meaning of psychoanalytic interpretations and then I shall discuss the distinction between description and explanation, that is, MacIntyre's standard for evaluating the explanatory power of any theory pretending to be scientific.

MACINTYRE ON THE MEANING OF PSYCHOANALYTIC INTERPRETATIONS

(a) Is Repression Unobservable?

MacIntyre's support of (a) is that repression is always inferred from subsequent behavior and feelings; it can never be observed in oneself—in the present, MacIntyre probably means, the way we might observe ourselves suppressing an impulse.[15] It is another question whether we can ever observe others repressing in the present. That we cannot does not follow from the impossibility of the first person case, as MacIntyre supposes. This is clear if we consider the analogous case of inadvertent actions. The impossibility of someone's observing himself doing something inadvertently does

15 Ibid., 70.

not entail the impossibility of his observing someone else doing something in that way. It is hard to avoid the impression that MacIntyre regards the unobservability of repression to be so obvious as to need no serious argument — as if even Freud would grant the point. Did Freud think that repression was unobservable? Here is a passage implying a negative answer, at least in the context of free association:

> In carrying out the technique of psycho-analysis, we continually require the patient to produce such derivatives of the repressed as, in consequence either of their remoteness or of their distortion, can pass the censorship of the unconscious. Indeed, the associations which we require him to give without being influenced by any conscious purposive idea and without any criticism, and from which we reconstitute a conscious translation of the repressed representative — these associations are nothing else than remote and distorted derivatives of this kind. During this process we observe that the patient can go on spinning a thread of such associations, till he is brought up against some thought, the relation of which to what is repressed becomes so obvious that he is compelled to repeat his attempt at repression. Neurotic symptoms, too, must have fulfilled this same condition, for they are derivatives of the repressed, which has, by their means, finally won the access to consciousness which was previously denied to it.[16]

The patient is compelled to repeat his attempt at repression before our eyes. If he succeeds, we will have observed the repression of some thought, though without necessarily knowing what thought has been repressed. The passage quoted here brings out the extreme importance of free association in fixing the sense of Freud's other concepts. MacIntyre ignores this in defining repression as well as the unconscious, as we shall see. Because he ignores the peculiarities of free association in defining these concepts, it is not surprising that, in his view, the only role free association has for the patient should be explainable as follows: "For the patient there is an alternation between identification — the recognition of what he is doing and feeling — and the transformation by association, by working through

16. Freud, "Repression," 14:149–50.

his emotional states, of his attitudes and impulses."[17] Here, the work of free association is contrasted with that of recognition, as if it were not the sole means allowing analyst and patient to observe and identify what the patient is unconsciously doing. Even for the analyst, free association plays no role in recognition but merely serves to confirm interpretations reached by other means:

> The patient for example shows a wish to leave the room suddenly. The analyst interprets this by suggesting that the patient fears his own impulse to kill the analyst. The patient denies vehemently that he has any such impulse and perhaps a flow of highly excited free association follows. (This is what the analyst normally takes as confirming an interpretation as, if not entirely correct, at least near the mark.) . . . But our description of the development of the analysis is so far incomplete because it lacks any account of why the psychoanalyst offers the interpretations he does, of what it is that goes on in his mind. To consider this will be to bring out features of Freudian theory which are important for my purpose in this essay.
>
> The analyst's first step is to identify the behaviour. He sees its unconscious motivation in the sense that he sees it as an expression of fear of what the patient may do. He sees the purpose in the act which the patient does not see. How such unconscious purposes may be ascribed has already been made clear and of this we need therefore say no more. The analyst then explains the patient's inability to recognize this by postulating a conflict between an impulse which is directed against him and an impulse to suppress the former impulse to the extent of not admitting it. He then by means of his interpretation and the patient's response to it enables these impulses to become conscious.[18]

How the analyst is able to identify the behavior at the start as an expression of fear at what the patient may do, apart from the associations of the patient and how the analyst sees "the purpose in the act which the patient does not see" are not really explained here; the problem, for the analyst, is that of correctly characterizing the self-deceptive conduct of the patient, whose associations serve merely as confirmation of interpretations already arrived at (presumably, by

17. MacIntyre, *The Unconscious*, 66.
18. Ibid., 64–66.

means of those correlations MacIntyre alludes to in (1) and (2)), and to aid the patient in "working through his emotional states."

Now free association is a kind of behavior no one before Freud seems to have paid much attention to. It is a new language-game, I am tempted to say. It supplies a whole new sort of evidence, and a new kind of experience for the patient. If it is even possible that in free association repression becomes observable, whereas outside it repression (normally) must be inferred, then much light would be thrown, not only on limitations in MacIntyre's conception of repression and his certainty that it is unobservable, but also on his wholly unexamined concept of unobservability. In order to make plausible such a strong connection between repression and free association, MacIntyre's own definition (in (b)) is the main obstacle that would have to be removed, since it includes no such connection at all. Is (b) an adequate definition of repression?

(b) Defining Repression Operationally

MacIntyre's operational definition of repression (b) is defective in several ways. Strain and anxiety are not merely correlated with the inability to recall, in cases of repression. The strain and anxiety are related to what is repressed, to what the memory is a memory of, to its content; the content is what causes the anxiety. The strain and anxiety are not about the inability to recall but about what one is unable to recall. MacIntyre's operational definition of repression is satisfied as well by false cases — for example, quiz program contestants anxiously straining to recall the correct answer to the $64,000 question — as by genuine cases of repression, in which the forgotten idea seems alien to the person and is resisted. (In the case of the quiz program contestant, the strain and anxiety solely concern the difficulty and importance, to the contestant, of recalling.) In addition, it is not always the case that strain and anxiety vanish when the repressed memory is recalled, as MacIntyre's analysis requires: they may increase. Besides, MacIntyre seems to be committed to more than a mere correlation between the inability to recall and strain and anxiety; since the cessation of anxiety follows upon the recall of the forgotten memory, it must be the inability to recall that causes the anxiety, in his view. This is the reverse of the psychoanalytic concept, however, in which anxiety over certain ideas causes them to be forgotten. What MacIntyre's operational definition of repression fails to include is brought out by the following passage from Freud, who writes of patients who could not remember certain distressing things but then recalled them vividly: "It was a question of things which the patient wished to forget, and therefore intentionally repressed from his conscious thought and inhibited and suppressed."[19] The wish to forget constitutes repression, an idea that MacIntyre omits.

Now wishes are peculiar psychical phenomena, unlike wants or intentions. It is possible to wish for something that one knows or believes to be impossible. There are idle wishes, but no idle wants or intentions. Hence, wishes do not, need not, result in any particular goal-directed behavior. By contrast, if one wants X, there must be some conditions possible in which one believes that X can be obtained and in which one would do what is needed to get X. No such claim can be made concerning wishes. One need not try to obtain what one wishes for, even if one believes that it is possible to achieve it. Thus, there are no behavior patterns connected with wishing for X as there are behavior patterns associated with wanting or intending X. As a result, speaking of animals having wishes is problematic, since no behavior unlinked to self-ascription appears to be capable of serving as a criterion of a creature's having a certain wish. So what makes the question whether repression is unobservable hard to answer may be a feature it shares with many conscious mental phenomena—namely, repression is concerned with a subject's wishes concerning himself. Since wishes do not relate to actions in a systematic way, it is at least going to be harder to observe them than wants or intentions. The distinction between wishes and wants is of course a categorical distinction in place in our language independent of Freud. The reason why we cannot ascribe repression to a subject on the basis of behavior apart from free association or what the subject would assent to may be nothing more mysterious than the fact that

19. Freud, *Studies on Hysteria,* 2:10.

repression necessarily involves the wishes of the subject, and wishes quite generally cannot be ascribed to subjects on the basis of behavior unlinked to assent.[20] So the difficulty with repression would then be one shared by all psychic phenomena concerned with wishes, whether conscious or unconscious; it would then be not the unconsciousness of repression that makes it hard if not impossible to observe, but merely the fact that repression involves wishes. If we press the question whether repression is observable, the answer must depend in part on whether wishes are observable, whether conscious wishes are observable — and here there seems to be a dilemma for MacIntyre. If he agrees that conscious wishes are observable by others, for example, when the subject ascribes wishes to himself or assents to their ascription to himself, then it is hard to see how unconscious wishes differ in any relevant way. We would then have to say that unconscious wishes are observable, too, and so repression would be conceivably observable as well. On the other hand, if MacIntyre denies that conscious wishes are observable on the ground that the only criterion for others to ascribe them to subjects is the subjects' assent or self-ascription, then unconscious wishes would be unobservable, too, and so, too, would repression. But then, unobservability would have lost its stigma, since mental phenomena about which problems have not been raised, that is, conscious wishes, share the properties that MacIntyre refers to in casting doubt on the explanatory power of such concepts as repression. The claim on which this argument rests, namely, that unconscious wishes are similar to conscious ones in all relevant respects except that unconscious wishes require free association to gain assent, has been denied by Ernest Nagel:

> Unconscious motives have an enduring character and tenacious attachment to specific objectives that conscious wishes do not exhibit. Indeed, on Freudian theory a thwarted wish of early childhood, directed toward some person, may not completely vanish, but may enjoy a repressed

20. For contrasting treatments of the significance (and correctness) of Freud's assumptions about *wishing*, see Wollheim, *Sigmund Freud* and *Thread of Life*, and Cavell *Psychoanalytic Mind*.

existence in the unconscious, and continue to operate in identical form into the present even though that person has long since died.* In consequence, there is an important failure of analogy between conscious motives and unconscious mental processes, so that it is only by a radical shift in the customary meanings of such words as "motive" and "wish" that Freudian theory can be said to offer an explanation of human conduct in terms of motivations and wish-fulfillments.

*Cf. "The Unconscious" [This is a specific reference to *S.E.* 14: 186–87].[21]

Nagel's example hardly provides any argument for his point at all; it is possible to have the conscious wish, for example, to ask some question of a person out of one's childhood, even though the person has long since died and the wisher knows that they have died. (The subject may also consciously wish they were alive in order for the other wish to be realized.) In this respect, conscious wishes do not differ from unconscious ones. The only way to make it come out that Nagel is right about the supposed disanalogy is to assume that such wishes as I have indicated are impossible or unintelligible, which they are not.

Clearly, in addition to the problem arising from the peculiarities of wishing, the question of the observability of repression is beset by the lack of clarity in the concept of unobservability, which we do not know how to apply to wishes. Neither MacIntyre nor any other author I am aware of has provided correspondence rules for applying unobservability, nor is it easy to see how unobservability — or for that matter, observability — might be given such an operational definition. These two problems appear, compounded, when we turn to examine (c), the question of whether what is repressed is unobservable — that is, whether the contents of the unconscious are unobservable.

(c) Is the Unconscious Unobservable?

These questions cannot be answered until we determine what is repressed, what is in the unconscious. For Freud, the answers

21. Nagel, "Methodological Issues in Psychoanalytic Theory," 45.

to both questions are the same — it is ideas that get repressed; it is ideas that the unconscious contains.

> In our discussion so far we have dealt with the repression of an instinctual representative, and by the latter we have understood an idea or group of ideas which is cathected with a definite quota of psychical energy (libido or interest) coming from an instinct.[22]

> We have said that there are conscious and unconscious ideas; but are there also unconscious instinctual impulses, emotions and feelings, or is it in this instance meaningless to form combinations of this kind?

> I am in fact of the opinion that the antithesis of conscious and unconscious is not applicable to instincts. An instinct can never become an object of consciousness — only the idea that represents the instinct can. Even in the unconscious, moreover, an instinct cannot be represented otherwise than by an idea. . . . When we nevertheless speak of an unconscious instinctual impulse or of a repressed instinctual impulse, the looseness of phraseology is a harmless one. We can only mean an instinctual impulse the ideational representative of which is unconscious, for nothing else comes into consideration.

> We should expect the answer to the question about unconscious feelings, emotions and affects to be just as easily given. It is surely of the essence of an emotion that we should be aware of it, i.e., that it should become known to consciousness. Thus the possibility of the attribute of unconsciousness would be completely excluded as far as emotions, feelings and affects are concerned. . . . In general, the use of the terms 'unconscious affect' and 'unconscious emotion' has reference to the vicissitudes undergone, in consequence of repression, by the quantitative factor in the instinctual impulse. . . . Strictly speaking, then, and although no fault can be found with the linguistic usage, there are no unconscious affects as there are unconscious ideas.[23]

Now just as wishes differ categorically from wants and intentions, ideas — thoughts — differ from beliefs and assumptions. Thoughts or ideas that one knows to be false can pass through one's mind. Such ideas need not affect one's conduct in any specific way, whereas beliefs always do. If one believes that X, there must be some condi-

22. Freud, "Repression," 14:152.
23. Freud, "The Unconscious," 14:177–78.

tions possible (depending on one's wants) in which one's conduct will be altered by one's belief that X. Thus, there are no specific behavior patterns connected with having ideas as there are with beliefs or assumptions. Again, it is problematic to speak of animals having ideas, since no behavior unlinked to self-ascription appears to be capable of serving as criterion of a creature's having certain ideas. By contrast, beliefs can be ascribed to animals; a cat may think the mouse it chased into a hole is still there, when we know it is not, for example. So it makes no sense to speak of the unconscious of an animal, it seems; since animals have no wishes or ideas, they have no unconscious ones either.

Pretty clearly, the same sort of problem having to do with these peculiarities in the concept of ideas will arise when we try to decide whether the unconscious is unobservable. Ideas cannot be ascribed to subjects completely apart from their own self-ascriptions or from their assent to such ascriptions when others propose them. This is certainly true of conscious ideas; behavior wholly independent of assent or self-ascription cannot be the criterion of ascribing conscious ideas to people. If we ask whether conscious ideas are observable in others, the question is mysterious — it presumably means, does our hearing a person say sincerely (so that we believe him) that he has a certain idea at a certain instant count as our observing his idea? One is tempted to think that it either does or does not — and as before, a problem arises for MacIntyre whatever we say. For if our hearing him thus does count as observing his idea, then unconscious ideas are observable, too, since our criterion for ascribing them is also self-ascription or assent. If we say that in such a situation we have not really observed his conscious idea, then conscious ideas are unobservable, and thus unconscious ideas are not unusual in their unobservability; unobservability can no longer count as a point against taking unconscious ideas seriously if we continue to take conscious ideas seriously. We should probably avoid saying anything to such a strange question as Are other people's conscious ideas observable? and begin to pay more attention to the oddness, indeed, absurdity of the question, and to the strangeness of the concept *unobservability*. I shall return to these topics later in discussing

MacIntyre's standard by which the explanatory power of any theory is to be judged.

(d) The Operational Definition of Unconscious Motivation

As we would expect, the crucial absence of reference to ideas in MacIntyre's treatment of the unconscious recurs in his operational definition of the meaning of statements ascribing unconscious motives to subjects, that is, in his operational definition of unconscious ambition. MacIntyre introduces the account already quoted with the following remark: "When we ascribe an intention, purpose or motive to someone, we do more than assert a tendency to behave in a particular way or a pattern in their actions. . . . It always makes sense to say that Smith seems to be ambitious, because he behaves in certain ways, but that he may not in fact be ambitious; it would be nonsense to say of salt that it dissolved and would therefore seem to be soluble but might not be." First of all, it is hard to see why MacIntyre thinks that "if Smith denied his ambition, the onus would be on him to provide us with a plausible alternative explanation of his behaviour,"[24] if the distinction made here between ambition and solubility is correct. Why is the onus not on us to explain why Smith seems ambitious to us?

The distinction MacIntyre seeks to draw between ambition and solubility is far from clear; the matter is partly obscured by the fact that ambition is certainly not an intention or purpose, though it may be a motive. If a person behaves in those ways that are prima facie good evidence that he is ambitious, it still makes sense to say that he only appears to be ambitious, but is not really so. If we are going to say, of a person who behaves in those ways that are prima facie good evidence that he is ambitious, that he only seems ambitious, it is going to have to be because he did not really behave in the ways we thought he did but only seemed to. Thus, if over a period of years, Smith eagerly urges his friends to nominate him for every political office for which he is eligible, enthusiastically campaigns for each election, and serves with pleasure when elected, we may say he is

24. MacIntyre, *The Unconscious*, 57–58.

ambitious. Nothing further Smith may say about himself can negate this judgment, unless it be to show that it was not he who urged his friends to nominate him as appeared, or that his eagerness in doing so was not what it appeared; that it was not he who campaigned as we thought, or that his enthusiasm for it was faked; that it was not he who served, as it seemed, or that his pleasure in serving was not genuine. It cannot be that he did urge them, campaign, and serve as appeared but is not really ambitious.

A plausible objection would be the following: suppose Smith only did all those things that are prima facie good evidence of ambition because, for example, mobsters threatened to kill him if he did not. Suppose further that the interests he sought to advance when in office were not his own but those of the people threatening him. Then, he was not really ambitious but only seemed so; yet he did do all those things counted as prima facie good evidence of ambition. This is confused, however; if he did act under duress, then his eagerness, enthusiasm, and pleasure were not genuine. If they were real, he did not act under duress. It is of course possible to launch a person who is not ambitious to start with on a political career through threats of violence. But then we have explained how he came to be ambitious, genuinely, though he was not so to start with. We have not then rebutted the claim that he is ambitious.

MacIntyre's salt example is similar to his ambition case; if the salt dissolves in water, it is soluble. The only way to avoid the inference is to show that the salt did not really dissolve but only seemed to, or that it was not really salt, or that the substance it dissolved in was not really water. Of course, there are many more ways for someone to seem ambitious but not really be so than there are ways for salt to seem soluble but not really be so. Nevertheless, ambition, like any motive, is the sort of thing for which the subject's conduct can provide prima facie good evidence for ascribing the motive to him. Besides, the psychological factor, if there is one, in virtue of which some case of apparent ambition is confirmed as genuine because of its presence, or rejected as illusory because of its absence, is never an idea in the mind of the subject. If Smith denies he is ambitious, after fulfilling the conditions that are prima facie good evidence of ambition, we could say he is deceived about himself; the same applies to vanity, greed, cruelty, pride, envy, and many other character traits that also double as motives. Like ambition, they can be predicated of a subject regardless of whether he predicates them of himself or assents if asked. If someone does the sorts of things ambitious people do and denies he is ambitious, this does not necessarily undermine our judgment. It may merely show that he is self-deceived, rationalizing, ignorant of what the word means, completely oblivious to his own actions, or whatever. What it cannot be taken to show is the failure of some idea to be present in his mind consciously, or the presence of some idea in his mind, unconsciously. It follows that no idea is at all essential to the presence of ambition in him, since as we have already seen, the presence of an idea in a subject assumes his assent (or linkage to assent) or self-ascription as criterion. The point that no particular ideas are essential to the presence of a motivating trait such as ambition is even clearer if we consider other cases, such as envy, laziness, cruelty. It would be out of bounds to claim that what we mean when we ascribe these motives to people involves in each case the presence in their minds of some idea — that is why we can predicate such motives of others without their assent as criterion, almost as surely as we can predicate solubility of salt upon observing its dissolution.

So MacIntyre's operational definition of unconscious ambition is either not really a description of any possible case of ambition at all, if the conduct it describes is defined as a case of unconsciousness of something, or it is not really a case of a man unconscious of something about himself, if he is really ambitious, or else Smith is neither ambitious nor unconscious of something about himself in the acts in question. Smith's awareness — or lack of awareness — of his own ambitiousness cannot be relevant to his being consciously or unconsciously ambitious, since if he is genuinely ambitious, then what he can be unconscious of is not that — for no idea is constitutive of ambition. That is, being ambitious does not involve merely having some idea, nor is it having an idea *plus* something else, either; the having of an idea is not a necessary condition of ambition. What MacIntyre's subject lacks is knowledge of his own actions, the sort of thing others might know about him, independent of his assent.

On the other hand, if he is unconscious of something, it is not his ambition, since no idea is constitutive of ambition, and whatever he is unconscious of must be an idea, the sort of thing others cannot ascribe to him completely independent of his own assent or self-ascription. Simply put, what is unconscious is an idea; what motivates action is never an idea (though it may be a belief). Of course, nothing said so far implies that unconscious ambition cannot exist. What is implied is that if there is such a thing as unconscious ambition, its operational definition cannot be the one MacIntyre supplies, nor can it be any other definition omitting mention of some unconscious idea as an essential part of it. A genuine case of unconscious ambition cannot be one in which the subject simply does not know something about his own conduct, for example, that it is ambitious conduct. In fact, a genuine case of unconscious ambition would just as likely be one in which the subject does not behave ambitiously at all. Only if it can be shown of the subject that certain ideas that would manifest ambition if acted upon are present in him would it be plausible to ascribe unconscious ambition to him. Thus, a point similar to the one MacIntyre tried but failed to make about ambition in contrast to solubility is correct for unconscious wishes and ideas, indeed, for wishes and ideas quite generally. That is, behavior patterns independent of assent are not connected with wishes and ideas as prima facie good evidence for their presence, whereas such behavior patterns are present for ambition and other motives. A person can unconsciously fear his father (to switch to MacIntyre's other example) without behaving in any characteristic way. If there were characteristic behavior patterns for unconscious fear of one's father, the assent of the subject would not be needed to establish it. A man who is unconsciously afraid of his father may behave contemptuously or indifferently in his father's presence. We can ascribe unconscious fear of father to someone who is bluff, hearty, or insolent around his father, or who avoids his father, or who is never around his father, or even to someone whose father is long dead. It is not a necessary condition of unconscious fear of one's father that one act fearfully when in his presence. MacIntyre seems to assume that unconscious fear of father is behaviorally exactly like conscious fear of father, except that the consciousness of one's fear is absent in the former. But this account is wrong from the start; for what constitutes conscious fear is certain behavior, not any particular idea, whereas what constitutes unconscious fear are certain ideas, not any behavior. (Even if a person has feelings of fear around his father, he may not be afraid of his father. Such feelings, like ideas, are not necessarily connected to any behavior, whereas being afraid is.) Thus far, MacIntyre's definition of unconscious ambition (or unconscious fear of one's father) does not offer a necessary condition of these states. His definition does not provide even a sufficient condition either, as can be seen from the fact that it is a simple matter to construct a case satisfying MacIntyre's operational definition of unconscious fear of one's father, but in which that is not what any psychoanalyst would find. Suppose that to others Smith behaves in ways that seem to indicate his fear of his father, cannot plausibly explain his fearful-seeming behavior otherwise, cannot recognize his own fear of his father when it is pointed out to him, and vehemently denies he is afraid of his father. Smith's behavior may nevertheless actually manifest unconscious fear of his mother, whom he fantasizes to be envious of his attachment to his father. Smith may behave in ways that seem fearful of his father when he is in his father's presence, be unable to explain this behavior otherwise, deny he is afraid of his father, but not be unconsciously afraid of his father. What Smith does unconsciously fear might be his own attachment to his father, the danger of his father becoming attached to him, because he is afraid of his mother's disapproval. (Needless to say, an indefinite number of other accounts are possible that would fit the description of Smith's behavior as well as the one offered here.)

Why does MacIntyre propose the account of unconscious ambition that he does, in which it is presented as the behavior constitutive of conscious ambition minus the consciousness of one's own behavior? Such an account can be expected if motivation quite generally is assumed to be modelled on intention or purpose; this MacIntyre does assume, it seems, insofar as motivation, like intention, requires avowal, he thinks. Of Smith, who behaves ambitiously, he writes:

> Asking Smith himself is not the only thing that would be relevant. We would watch his further behaviour and the extent to which he behaved consistently. But the crucial test would still be Smith's response when we

asked him about his ambition. . . . Both elements of intentional action —
the pattern in the behaviour and the possibility of avowal, are essential in
both the ordinary and the Freudian applications of the concepts of motive
and intention. All those cases in which philosophers have seen an intention which is *only* a pattern of behaviour are cases where the agent would
avow the intention if certain conditions were fulfilled. And thus the fact
that his intention may not actually occur as a piece of conscious mental
activity is irrelevant. What matters is what would happen *if* the agent
were to be pressed on the matter.[25]

The assimilation of motivation to intention, purpose, seems
wrong; there is no reason why individuals motivated by cruelty or
laziness, for example, might not rationalize, deceive themselves
about their motives indefinitely, no matter how long or hard they are
pressed. Yet the attribution of these motives to them by others need
not be withdrawn merely on that account. Indeed, as Anthony Kenny
remarks: "It is possible to act from a motive without possessing any
concept of the motive from which one acts; as it is not possible to act
for a purpose without a concept of the purpose for which one acts.
Caesar's style in the *De Bello Gallico* can be clearly seen to have been
motivated by lifemanship; but he cannot have possessed a concept
which was invented only in our own time."[26] However, if motives are
thought of as intentions (in requiring the possibility of avowal) as
MacIntyre supposes and if there are cases of people whose behavior is
the same as those who avow motives such as ambition, except that
they are not aware of such motives in themselves, it will seem necessary to ascribe awareness of their motives to them in some sense, since
even such motives would have to be like intentions, that is, capable of
being avowed. Saying such people are unconsciously ambitious
would then be a way of satisfying the (false) principle that motives

25. Ibid., 58–59.
26. Kenny, *Action, Emotion and Will*, 87. The inventor of "lifemanship"
is the satirist Stephen Potter, who writes by way of defining the term: *"How
to be one up* — how to make the other man feel that something has gone
wrong, however slightly. The Lifeman is never caddish himself, but how
simply and certainly, often, he can make the other man feel a cad, and over
prolonged periods" (*Lifemanship*, xiv).

can always be avowed by those in whom they are truly to be found. It is because MacIntyre subscribes to such a principle (and to the idea that motives are intentions) that he finds it natural to operationally define unconscious ambition as he does, it seems. He is obliged to say something about cases of people who behave ambitiously but who deny they are ambitious, something which he would not feel obliged to say if he did not assimilate motives in general to intentions. If we assume motives are not intentions, nothing at all needs to be said about such cases. For on that assumption, nothing about the ascription of motives requires that those in whom motives are to be found must be aware of their motives, must be capable of avowing them. This distortion in his conception of motives (as intentions) is also responsible for MacIntyre's misunderstanding of what it is that unconscious motives are supposed to explain; he assumes that "The unconscious explains the continuity between infancy and adult life,"[27] which I will now examine.

(e) What Does Unconscious Mental Activity Explain?

Certainly, if we assume (i) that unconscious motives are properly defined operationally as MacIntyre claims and (ii) that motives are intentions, we can also see that the continuity between childhood and adult life does not need explanation in terms of unconscious motives. For (i) and (ii) require that we can only ascribe unconscious motives when the sort of behavior is present that a subject could avow a conscious motive for. Now correlations, continuities of the sort in question, are not behavior for which anyone would ever avow a conscious motive. There are no conscious motives for which such continuities are the relevant behavior (in the way certain behavior patterns are relevant to ambition, for example). So, of course, such continuities are also not capable of bearing explanation by unconscious motives, either. MacIntyre's claim that such continuities do not need unconscious motives for their explanation is thus too weak; given (i) and (ii), such continuities cannot be explained by unconscious motives, since they are incapable of explanation by conscious motives, as MacIntyre defines these. It is, of

27. MacIntyre, *The Unconscious*, 70.

course, possible for a person to have as a conscious motive "reproducing a childhood situation in adult action"; compare MacIntyre's reference to "the original traumatic childhood situation which his [the neurotic's] adult actions are reproducing."[28] This reference, however, is problematic considering MacIntyre's account of unconscious motivation, for the behavior of neurotics is not behavior on the basis of which such a conscious motive can be ascribed. Someone consciously seeking to reproduce a childhood situation would surely not resort to any of the odd, indirect, vaguely related actions neurosis involves—he would do what he did in childhood *again*. In this respect, MacIntyre is mistaken to claim that neurotic behavior is "behaviour of a kind appropriate to certain key situations in early childhood."[29] For the term *appropriate* in this sentence cannot be given any operational definition, it seems.

MacIntyre's assumption that motives are intentions is thus crucial to his conclusion that unconscious motives are not needed to explain child/adult correlations, as well as to his peculiar account (in '[d] The Operational Definition of Unconscious Motivation" above) of unconscious motives as involving avowal as a necessary condition. Is MacIntyre correct to suppose that Freud introduced the concepts of repression and unconscious motivation in order to explain child/adult correlations? As a general claim, correlations between events in early life and adult experience are universal among normal as well as abnormal humans, among animals, and even among plants. Often such correlations in humans do not involve any forgetting or wish to forget at all on their part, and so repression can hardly then share in their explanation, especially if MacIntyre's definition of repression is adopted. Even if we restrict the scope of the claim to those correlations to be found in the lives of neurotic human beings, it is hard to see what repression could explain, since many such correlations are and have always been conscious to them. Besides, Freud is clear that what repression is intended to explain is not the mere correlation between child and adult, even the neurotic child and adult, but the resistance and transference phenomena that

28. Ibid., 64.
29. Ibid.

may be observed as often as one pleases if one undertakes an analysis of a neurotic without resorting to hypnosis. In such cases one comes across a resistance which opposes the work of analysis and in order to frustrate it pleads a failure of memory. The use of hypnosis was bound to hide this resistance; the history of psycho-analysis, proper, therefore, only begins with the new technique that dispenses with hypnosis. The theoretical consideration of the fact that this resistance coincides with an amnesia leads inevitably to the view of unconscious mental activity which is peculiar to psycho-analysis and which, too, distinguishes it clearly from philosophical speculations about the unconscious. It may thus be said that the theory of psycho-analysis is an attempt to account for two striking and unexpected facts of observation which emerge whenever an attempt is made to trace the symptoms of a neurotic back to their sources in his past life: the facts of transference and of resistance. Any line of investigation which recognizes these two facts and takes them as the starting-point of its work has a right to call itself psycho-analysis, even though it arrives at results other than my own. But anyone who takes up other sides of the problem while avoiding these two hypotheses will hardly escape a charge of misappropriation of property by attempting impersonation, if he persists in calling himself a psycho-analyst.[30]

The implication here seems clearly that if neurotics had shown no resistance or transference when one had attempted to trace their symptoms, then the introduction of the concepts of repression and the unconscious would not have been justified, according to Freud, even if the correlations between adult symptom and childhood experience still existed. (It is the discontinuities, not the continuities, that Freud seeks above all to explain.)

Failure to recognize resistance and transference as the central data upon which the concepts of repression and the unconscious rest is responsible for a common criticism of psychoanalysis, which is that it makes no predictions and therefore cannot be verified. (MacIntyre's criticism is a variant of this, although he thinks there are predictions that can be made on the supposition that the unconscious exists; his point is that these same predictions can be arrived at without that assumption just as well.) Karl Popper makes the objection in its more usual form when he writes of his growing realiza-

30. Freud, *On the History of the Psycho-Analytic Movement,* 14:16.

tion, beginning in 1919, that psychoanalytic theories were "simply non-testable, irrefutable. There was no conceivable human behaviour which could contradict them."[31] According to Popper, "every conceivable case could be interpreted in the light of" Freud's theory, a claim he illustrates "by two very different examples of human behaviour: that of a man who pushes a child into the water with the intention of drowning it; and that of a man who sacrifices his life in an attempt to save the child. Each of these two cases can be explained with equal ease in Freudian . . . terms. According to Freud the first man suffered from repression (say, of some component of his Oedipus complex), while the second man had achieved sublimation."[32] Apparently, what psychoanalysis is supposed to explain, according to Popper, is how it is possible for human beings to have both actions as possible behaviors, or why, quite generally, some people drown children, and others save them from drowning. The claim that repression *explains* one person's drowning a child and sublimation explains rescuing another is fantastic, especially when ascribed to Freud. It is extraordinary that Popper supposes he can make up cases and guess what a psychoanalyst (any psychoanalyst) would say about them — which already settles the nonscientific nature of the example; it is an imaginary example of a supposedly scientific explanation. The questions are absurd, however: Why do some people save children from drowning? Why do some people drown children? As if any and all people who do these things share common motives — that is, as if drowning a child were behavior characteristic of some motive.

A more serious problem concerns whether Popper really illustrates or supports his general claim. His general claim, "(i) psychoanalytic theory is non-testable," has not been established merely by claiming that "(ii) any and all possible behavior can be explained by psychoanalytic interpretation," even if we suppose that Popper's examples of interpretation are genuine. To illustrate the truth of (i) Popper would have to show that the supposedly Freudian claim,

31. Popper, *Conjectures and Refutations,* 37.
32. Ibid., 35.

"(iii) people who drown children are suffering from repression of some Oedipus complex component" is nontestable, nonfalsifiable. For if (iii) is falsifiable, then (ii) is one step closer to being capable of being false, and (i) has a counterexample. But Popper does not even try to prove that (iii) cannot be tested; he simply assumes it. That (iii) is unfalsifiable is by no means obvious; indeed, (iii) would seem to be one of those child/adult correlations that needs no theory at all to confirm or disprove it, according to MacIntyre. Popper has not illustrated what he claimed to, then.[33] For Popper to say of a theory that it explains everything (that is, all possible behavior) is, no doubt, to claim that it is unfalsifiable, untestable. Then (i) and (ii) mean the same thing; but are they true? Only if (iii) is untestable.

William P. Alston tries to make the same point as Popper's when he writes: "It is easy to get the impression that a plausible explanation in psychoanalytic terms could be framed for any behavior, no matter what the facts. If it is not a reaction-formation from overattachment to mother, then it is a projection of a self-directed death wish, and so on."[34] Partly, his doubts rest on the possibility that psychoanalytic theory "can provide only suggestions for retrospective explanations," and that it does not

> yield general hypotheses to the effect that whenever strong desires of a certain kind are met with strong internal and/or external opposition, then (perhaps with the further assumption of certain kinds of intervening experiences) abnormal symptoms of certain kinds will be forthcoming. In other words, since unconscious psychic processes are supposed to provide connecting links between observables, a theory about them should imply that certain antecedent observables would lead to certain consequent observables.

33. Popper may have lost his way in his own argument; the text from which these quotes are taken tries to show that Freud's theory, *as well as Adler's theory,* is nontestable, since each explains everything. Popper confuses the issue, it seems, of whether an alternative theory to Freud's explains things as well as Freud's does, with the issue of whether Freud's theory, or the alternative one, is falsifiable. The defect of untestability is supposed to be present in both, however.

34. Alston, "Psychoanalytic Theories, Logical Status of," 515.

> In fact, however, we find little of this. . . . Virtually nothing has been
> done to derive testable hypotheses specifying sufficient conditions for the
> occurrence of abnormal symptoms. It is only if this were done that the
> theory could be used for the prediction of such phenomena.[35]

Clearly, Alston, like MacIntyre, supposes that if psychoanalysis
were an explanation of anything, it would be an explanation of
symptom formation. By contrast, Freud's position might be stated
by saying that inquiry into symptom formation is impossible unless
resistance and transference phenomena are taken into account; in
addition, the explanation of these phenomena provides the basis
needed for explaining symptoms themselves. Besides, the question
of whether psychoanalysis makes any predictions can be met head
on here. For when the confusion is corrected (in the criticisms of
MacIntyre, Popper, and Alston) concerning what phenomena the
concepts of repression and the unconscious were introduced in order
to explain, and resistance, transference and the method of free association are moved to the foreground, we can see much to count as
prediction in psychoanalytic interpretation, plenty to count as verification or falsification of such predictions.

First of all, the very expression of an interpretation in words to the
patient is a prediction, namely, that the patient will assent to the
interpretation made. The analyst wants to make interpretations that
will be accepted and only offers those having a good chance of being
assented to. That offering an interpretation is the making of a prediction remains true in this limited sense, then, even if it is supposed
that no further verification or falsification of the interpretation is
possible. So an interpretation, even before it is made to the patient,
can be regarded as a prediction concerning what sorts of results free
association will produce. It says in what direction free association to
the elements of the dream, for example, will converge, it tells what
the dream is about. Once the associations of the dreamer are available, the interpretation is a prediction, at least concerning what the
subject will assent to. Of course, saying this can be misleading, since
it suggests that interpretations regularly precede free associations,

35. Ibid., 515, 514.

whereas associations are as likely to generate interpretations as corroborate them.

So far, MacIntyre's accounts of repression and the unconscious have been the main subjects of criticism, along with his conception of what sort of phenomena those concepts were meant to explain. Even if these views are accepted, however, a more serious problem arises when we consider the standards MacIntyre used to evaluate, not only psychoanalytic explanations, but any other explanations, however interpreted. To start with, MacIntyre sketches an account of scientific theory similar to that laid down by E. Nagel and quoted earlier in this chapter. MacIntyre writes:

> The basic requirement for a scientific theory is not that it shall refer to nothing but observables but that statements which are about observables and therefore verifiable by observation or experiment shall be deducible from it. But this is not enough. The theory must not merely be such that the statements concerning the regularities which it was originally introduced to explain are deducible from it. We must also be able if the explanation of the regularities with which we were originally concerned is correct, to deduce further statements of a testable kind, the verifying of which constitutes the confirmation of the hypothesis.[36]

The first sentence seems to indicate (somewhat obscurely) that MacIntyre feels the need for operational definitions of theoretical terms as strongly as Nagel does. (Besides, MacIntyre does provide what amount to operational definitions for both "repression" and "unconscious motive" as I have noted.) Trouble begins early on, as we have seen, when MacIntyre tries to apply this schema of scientific explanation to psychoanalysis: "Freud does not merely add to the list of mental states and events. He provides an explanation of those events and of their relation to the events of early childhood. In this explanation the term 'the unconscious,' which expresses a conceptual innovation by means of a linguistic one, has a key theoretical

36. MacIntyre, *The Unconscious*, 47.

role. So that we have not only to deal with 'unconscious' as a descriptive term, but with 'the unconscious' as an explanatory concept."[37]

The statement is too vague to be judged correct or not; although what MacIntyre means by it — that is, statement (e) — has already been criticized for its failure to include resistance and transference as the phenomena whose explanation justifies introducing repression and the unconscious as explanatory concepts (as opposed to the neurotic symptoms, inquiry into which reveals resistance and transference). But further difficulties emerge when MacIntyre objects to the hypothesis of the unconscious: "From the supposition of such an entity what consequences flow that could not otherwise be predicted? Freud's hypotheses as to the infantile origin of adult traits and disorders can all be formulated without reference to it."[38]

It is possible to interpret MacIntyre's critical requirement to mean:

> (f) the assumption of the existence of an unobservable entity, for example, the unconscious, is justified only if consequences follow from assuming it that cannot be predicted otherwise.

MacIntyre's second sentence seems to start from a different point, however: whether those consequences can be formulated without reference to the unconscious. This critical requirement might be put this way:

> (g) the assumption of the existence of an unobservable entity, for example, the unconscious, is justified only if the consequences that follow from it cannot be formulated without reference to it.

Now (g) would be an absurd requirement to adopt, since it denies a requirement of scientific theory MacIntyre has himself already accepted, namely, the need for all terms referring to unobservables to have operational definitions. Nevertheless, he apparently does go on to say that the trouble with the unconscious is that the causal expla-

37. Ibid., 49.
38. Ibid., 71–72.

nations generated by assuming its existence can all be formulated without reference to it. "My thesis then is that so far as Freud uses the concept of the unconscious as an explanatory concept, he fails, if not to justify it, at least to make clear its justification. He gives us causal explanations, certainly; but these can and apparently must stand or fall on their own feet without reference to it."[39] If we suppose MacIntyre really wanted to say that (f) is the test psychoanalysis fails, other difficulties arise. For (f) appears to be too strict a requirement for any scientific theory to satisfy. It is impossible to prove that even the best scientific theory is the only one capable of predicting certain results. At most, one is justified in demanding that a theory satisfy the following requirement:

> (h) the assumption of the existence of an unobservable entity, for example, the unconscious, is justified only if consequences follow from it that no plausible alternative theory predicts as well.

However, since MacIntyre offers no arguments to show that other theories predict "Freud's hypotheses as to the infantile origins of adult traits and disorders" as well as the assumption of the unconscious does, (h) is certainly not what he has in mind; indeed, MacIntyre denies that the unconscious has any explanatory role at all. His reason for saying this appears to be that "Freud's hypotheses" can be formulated as simple correlations between childhood and adult experience — and thus need no theory to explain them at all; mere induction is sufficient, MacIntyre seems to mean. Of such correlations MacIntyre writes: "Their being put forward is dependent on no particular background of theory. To test them is simply a matter of amassing evidence."[40] For MacIntyre, such correlations need no theory in order to be formulated, nor do they need any theory in order to be discovered.

It is possible to regard MacIntyre's argument as a reductio ad absurdum of one conception of what place theoretical (or unobserv-

39. Ibid., 72.
40. Ibid., 67.

able) entities have in scientific theories, rather than as a criticism of the psychoanalytic concept of the unconscious, for the argument would seem to lead to the rejection of all theoretical entities, none of which can be substituted in the following argument and survive:

1. The unconscious, an unobservable entity, generates hypotheses which either can or cannot be formulated without reference to it.
2. If we suppose these hypotheses cannot be formulated without reference to the unconscious, then the unconscious has not been operationally defined.
3. If we suppose these hypotheses can be formulated without reference to the unconscious, then the unconscious is unnecessary to explain them.

So the dilemma is by no means peculiar to MacIntyre or to theories concerning the status of the unconscious in psychoanalysis; as Dudley Shapere notes, commenting on the debate between the positivistic and the Feyerabend-Kuhn approaches to the philosophy of science:

> How are we to give an account of the scientific enterprise according to which observations (experience, data, evidence) will be both *independent* of theory (any theory?) and *relevant* thereto? The difficulty is that, *prima facie,* a tension exists between the two requirements, for independence seems to demand that the meanings of observation terms be totally pure of any theoretical infusion, whereas relevance seems to demand that they be permeated, at least to some extent, by theory.[41]

Obviously, the status of unobservable entities in scientific theories and, indeed, the notion of unobservability itself demands clarification.

UNOBSERVABILITY IN SCIENCE

The contrast between unobservable and observable entities (processes, properties) as employed by MacIntyre (and by Madison

41. Shapere, "Notes Toward a Post-Positivistic Interpretation of Science," 123–24.

as well) makes it difficult for him to take seriously the idea that the unconscious might be observable. Apparently, he assumes that the distinction between observable and unobservable is an ontological one, that is, if a process or property is unobservable, there is no possibility of its becoming observable — unobservability is its very essence; it is eternally and necessarily unobservable. Every property or process is *absolutely* unobservable or not; this property of properties or processes attaches to them independent of context, relative to no theory or situation. According to this interpretation, it is out of the question that a property or process unobservable relative to one theory or situation might become observable relative to another or that means should be found for making it observable. Yet science does not typically employ observability-unobservability in this ontological fashion. The roundness of the earth, the configuration of molecules in a crystal, are unobservable relative to certain observers, theories, situations but are observed, or can be made observable, relative to others.

I might say that for MacIntyre the statement "Property (or process) P is unobservable" is always necessarily true or necessarily false — whereas I suggest that it is at least sometimes contingently so. I have no idea (nor, I suspect, does MacIntyre) how to tell if a certain property or process is unobservable or not in the ontological or absolute sense. Yet it is only after deciding that repression and the unconscious are absolutely unobservable that MacIntyre finds them problematic, it seems.

According to Madison, repression has "as its main theoretical referent the idea of unobservable inner psychic forces interacting and producing a variety of observable effects."[42] But when he comes to list these observable effects, among them are "3. The presence of 'repressive defenses'" and "5. The presence of resistance in therapy."[43] In regard to 5, it is interesting to note that although Madison tends to treat resistance (unlike repression) as observable, Freud sometimes writes in ways that might be taken as implying that even resistance is unobservable:

42. Madison, *Freud's Concept of Repression and Defense*, 31; cf., 155.
43. Ibid., 154.

How are we to arrive at a knowledge of the unconscious? It is of course only as something conscious that we know it, after it has undergone transformation or translation into something conscious. Psycho-analytic work shows us every day that translation of this kind is possible. In order that this should come about, the person under analysis must overcome certain resistances — the same resistances as those which, earlier, made the material concerned into something repressed by rejecting it from the conscious.[44]

We call all the forces which oppose the work of cure the patient's "resistances."[45]

The objective indication of resistance is that his [the patient's] associations stop short or wander far away from the theme that is being discussed.[46]

Clearly, what Freud means by "resistances" in the first quote cannot be defined merely in terms of the patient's opposition to treatment — for that opposition is seen there as a manifestation of something intrapsychic that existed prior to the attempted treatment. In the second quote, some of the opposing forces will be inferred from what is observed in therapy but may not themselves be observed there. In the third quote, resistance might seem to be itself unobservable — its coordinating definition is stated instead. Madison is at least unclear concerning the observability of resistance; compare the passage quoted above[47] with the following:

On the most general level, "resistance" is the name given to the repression tendency when it operates in therapy. On a behavioral level, resistance refers to certain kinds of observable actions of the patient in therapy. On a conceptual level, resistance was conceived as a psychological force, a countercharge, in the patient that opposed the therapist's efforts to get him to remember in the early days of psychoanalysis and to cure him in the broadest later formulations. This counterforce is observable outside

44. Freud, "The Unconscious, 14:166.
45. Freud, *Question of Lay Analysis,* 20:223.
46. Freud, *New Introductory Lectures on Psycho-Analysis,* 22:68.
47. Madison, *Freud's Concept of Repression and Defense,* 31.

of therapy as well as in. The general name for all its manifestations became "anticathexis." "Resistance" is the special name for the anticathectic force as it appears specifically in the therapeutic situation. Resistance is unconscious, the patient being unaware of his opposition to the therapist's efforts to change him.[48]

Does Madison regard resistance as observable? That depends on how his talk of "levels" is taken. Besides, if we think of resistance as a form of repression, and if the latter is unobservable, the former will seem so, too. But Madison does want to say that resistance refers to "certain kinds of observable actions of the patient in therapy."

I do not mean to criticize Madison and MacIntyre for using the ontological distinction between observables and unobservables imprecisely; I object to their using it at all. For in order to know that a property or process is absolutely unobservable, one would need to know that *no* technique could possibly make the property or process experienceable. So, to judge the absolute unobservability of even one property or process, one would need to know all possible techniques. This seems clearly to be an absurd condition—one would need to know all possible techniques and know that they are all of them. If this is the necessary condition of any judgment of the absolute unobservability of even one property or process, then the absurdity of ever judging that a property or process is absolutely unobservable follows. Another way of putting this point is to say that it is absurd to suppose that there is any property or process whose observability (or unobservability) is essential to it—that is, it is absurd to suppose that any property or process is observable or unobservable in all possible worlds.

The account of the distinction between observables and unobservables sketched here is superficially close enough to one Carl Hempel has already expounded to deserve comparison and contrast, since they are fundamentally different. Hempel writes:

Now the concept of observability itself obviously is relative to the techniques of observation used. What is unobservable to the unaided senses may well be observable by means of suitable devices such as telescopes, microscopes, polariscopes, lie detectors, Gallup polls, etc. If by direct observation we mean such observational procedures as do not make use of auxiliary devices, then such property terms as 'black,' 'hard,' 'liquid,' 'cool,' and such relation terms as 'above,' 'between,' 'spatially coincident,' etc., might be said to refer to directly observable attributes; if observability is construed in a broader sense, so as to allow for the use of certain specified instruments or other devices, the concept of observable attribute becomes more comprehensive.[49]

Now it is unclear whether free association is to count as an "auxiliary device" in Hempel's sense or as an observational procedure that does not make use of auxiliary devices. For if it is an auxiliary device, what, in the way of direct observation, is it auxiliary to? If a lie detector is auxiliary to direct cross-examination of a subject, what analogous procedure is free association supposed to be auxiliary to? That there is no answer suggests that free association must be a sort of direct observation, if it is observation at all. The discomfort we naturally experience at either categorization of free association suggests that something deeper is wrong with the distinction on which it rests.

Certainly, the intent to relativize the concept of observability (and therefore of unobservability) to the techniques of observation used is close to the one I have already sketched. But Hempel does not do what he says he means to do. Not only is the concept of observability not relativized to the technique of observation used, the concept is not relativized at all. This is evident from the fact that certain properties are directly observable, according to Hempel, even though it is clear that in many instances auxiliary devices would have to be used to observe them; for example, that the material at the center of the earth is hard or liquid, black or red, will probably never be directly observed or observable. The category in which blackness, hardness, and other qualities are placed is arrived at independent of whether auxiliary devices are needed. Besides, Hempel does not consider the possibility that what is now observable only by means of auxiliary devices might become observable directly. In addition, if the claim to

49. Hempel, "Studies in the Logic of Confirmation," 22–23.

have relativized the concept *observability* to techniques of observation were realized, no properties could be classified as directly observable in themselves. That it is possible to classify as directly observable any properties at all belies the claim that the concept of observability has been relativized to anything. Instead of relativizing the concept of observability, Hempel has merely introduced a new absolute distinction — that between directly observable and not directly observable properties — in place of the old absolute distinction between observable and unobservable properties. But if, as I have argued, the concept of a property or process whose essence it is to be observable (or unobservable) is confused, then so, too, must be the concept of a property or process whose essence it is to be directly observable (or not). It is for this reason that the distinction in terms of which the "Theoretician's Dilemma" is formulated is defective right from the start.

> We will assume that the (extra-logical) vocabulary of empirical science, or of any of its branches, is divided into two classes: *observational terms* and *theoretical terms*. In regard to an observational term it is possible, under suitable circumstances, to decide by means of direct observation, whether the term does or does not apply to a given situation. . . . Theoretical terms, on the other hand, usually purport to refer to not directly observable entities and their characteristics. . . . The preceding characterization of the two vocabularies is obviously vague; it offers no precise criterion by means of which any scientific term may be unequivocally classified as an observational term or as a theoretical one. But no such precise criterion is needed here; the questions to be examined in this essay are independent of precisely where the dividing line between the terms of the observational and the theoretical vocabularies is drawn.
>
> 3. Why Theoretical Terms?
>
> The use of theoretical terms in science gives rise to a perplexing problem: Why should science resort to the assumption of hypothetical entities when it is interested in establishing predictive and explanatory connections among observables? Would it not be sufficient for the purpose, and much less extravagant at that, to search for a system of general laws mentioning only observables, and thus expressed in terms of the observational vocabulary alone?[50]

50. Hempel, "Theoretician's Dilemma," 178–79.

First of all, the vagueness of the distinction between observational and theoretical terms is not at issue; exactly where the line is to be drawn between the two does not matter. What does matter is whether there is any line at all to be drawn between sets of properties, if the distinction has been relativized to techniques of observation. Hempel's reference to science resorting to "the assumption of hypothetical entities" is also a problem. A natural retort would be that science does nothing of the kind; science may assume certain entities to exist, but such entities are never hypothetical entities, which is an expression exactly like "entities whose essence it is to exist noncategorically" in meaning or lack of it. It may seem that this comment exploits a mere verbal ambiguity in Hempel's remarks, since he clearly does want to say that "the existence of hypothetical entities with specified characteristics and interrelations, as assumed by a given theory, can be examined inductively in the same sense in which the truth of the theory itself can be examined, namely, by empirical tests of its V_B-consequences."[51] To see why there is more than a verbal ambiguity here, Hempel's "V_B-consequences" needs explanation.

For a given theory, T, the basic vocabulary, V_B, is a set of extralogical terms sharing no term with V_T, the theoretical vocabulary.[52] V_B may include observational terms, but it may also include disposition terms, such as "malleable," "elastic," "hungry," and "tired," and terms such as "iron," "silver," "electrical resistance," which are "well understood" even though they are "not strictly observational terms."[53] Then, empirical tests of the truth of the theory in terms of its consequences (as expressed in this basic vocabulary) will test the theory's "explanatory and predictive use," "systematic economy and heuristic fertility."[54]

But this account of the truth of theories as consisting merely in their consequences—that is, their use, economy, and fertility—

51. Ibid., 220.
52. Ibid., 208.
53. Ibid., 209.
54. Ibid., 222.

seems as misconceived as is the account of the existence of hypothetical entities it is supposed to clarify, since consequential truth is no clearer than hypothetical existence. After all, how will the truth of the claim that a theory has certain consequences be explained — in terms of *its* consequences? An infinite regress of a vicious sort looms here. Besides, what would be needed is consideration of *all* the consequences of a theory — which no criterion could establish had been taken into account. Even if we accept the account of the existence of hypothetical entities in terms of tests of their V_B consequences, however, Hempel's solution to the Theoretician's Dilemma leaves much to be desired. First of all, his expansion of V_B to include well-understood terms as well as observation terms in no way relativizes the distinctions between observable and unobservable or directly observable and not directly observable; he has merely added to the list of things that can be taken to confirm a theory. "Electrical resistance," no matter how well understood, will never become observable or directly observable: the same is true of iron and silver, it seems. Therefore, Hempel cannot explain what discovering the nonhypothetical (that is, real) existence of a theoretical entity would be without committing himself to the existence of properties whose essence it is to be observable (or not observable), directly observable (or not directly observable). For V_B has been defined in this way. But these are absurd properties. So, even though he intends to make it possible to speak of discovering whether a hypothetical entity really exists, he has not succeeded in doing so. Indeed, this should have been evident from the first formulation of the problem:[55] "Why should science resort to the assumption of hypothetical entities when it is interested in establishing predictive and explanatory connections among observables?" This question would be senseless unless it was assumed that hypothetical entities are unobservable in an absolute way; for if their unobservability were supposed to be the sort that can be transformed into observability, one obvious reason why science should assume their existence is surely that we expect to be able to observe the hypothetical entities to which the theoretical

55. Ibid., 179.

terms refer. But then, of course, the Theoretician's Dilemma could not even arise. In short, the way to prevent the Theoretician's Dilemma from even arising is to refuse to allow the absolute distinction between observation terms and theoretical terms and statements on which it rests.

To say this is to move in the same direction as Hilary Putnam's argument in "What Theories Are Not." However, there are differences between his view and mine which I shall emphasize. Putnam is mainly concerned with rebutting the idea that observation reports can "be identified on the basis of the vocabulary they do or do not contain." So whether observation terms, which apply to "publicly observable things and signify observable qualities of these things,"[56] are all the (extralogical) vocabulary contained in a report does not determine whether the report is an observation report. (Cf. Peter Achinstein's comment, "The point is simply that there is no special class of terms which must be used in describing what is observed."[57]) Part of Putnam's reason for saying this is that observation terms "have at least the possibility of applying to unobservables."[58] He continues: (A.) "(2) There is not even a single *term* of which it is true to say that it *could not* (without changing or extending its meaning) be used to refer to unobservables. 'Red,' for example, was so used by Newton when he postulated that red light consists of *red* corpuscles. [footnote omitted] In short: if an 'observation term' is a term which *can*, in principle, only be used to refer to observable things, then *there are no observation terms*."[59]

Besides, theoretical terms need not designate unobservables:

[B.] 'satellite' is, for example, a theoretical term (although the things it refers to are quite observable*) and 'dislikes' clearly is not.

*Carnap might exclude 'satellite' as an observation term, on the ground that it takes a comparatively long time to verify that something is a satellite with the naked eye, even if the satellite is close to the parent

56. Putnam, "What Theories Are Not," 216, cf. 220; 215.
57. Achinstein, "Problem of Theoretical Terms," 241.
58. Putnam, "What Theories Are Not," 218.
59. Ibid.

body (although this could be debated). However, 'satellite' cannot be excluded on the quite different ground that many satellites are too far away to see (which is the ground that first comes to mind) since the same is true of the huge majority of all *red* things.[60]

In addition, observation statements may contain theoretical terms, for example: (C.) " 'We also *observed* the creation of two electron-positron pairs.' "[61]

Each of Putnam's examples ought to give us pause, however. First of all, it is not accurate historically to attribute to Newton the view that red light consists of red corpuscles. As Newton wrote to Oldenburg, it is the "magnitude, strength or vigour" of light rays that "affect the sense with various colours according to their bignesse & mixture; the biggest with the strongest colours, Reds & Yellows."[62] Besides, all that will have been illustrated, even if we accept Putnam's example, is the intelligibility of applying an observation term such as "red" to unobservable entities like corpuscles. But the intelligibility of such applications, for example, in fairy tales, does not establish the appropriateness of such applications in science, which is at issue. After all, if corpuscles are invisible, how can they really have color at all? For Putnam's point to succeed, as I believe it does, we shall have to change the example; suppose, instead of *red* we apply *hard* to corpuscles, as Newton did when he wrote "All bodies seem to be composed of hard particles. . . . Even the rays of light seem to be hard bodies."[63] Unfortunately, this change seems to concede that *red* is a term that could not be used to refer to unobservables. That would be too strong a conclusion, however; for Putnam to be right, there is no need for all observation terms to be applicable to all unobservables. So even if *red* cannot apply to corpuscles, all that is necessary is that there be some unobservable entity to which *red* can be applied in science. Is there such an unobservable? I suppose the center of the sun is such an entity; it makes sense to say of it

60. Ibid., 219.
61. Ibid.
62. 7 December 1675; *Correspondence*, I:376, quoted in Westfall, "Development of Newton's Theory of Color," 356.
63. Newton, *Opticks*, query 31, p. 381.

that it is red hot, not blue or white, even though it is unobservable in the sense required. To return to the main point: *hard,* like *red,* signifies an observable property, but one which it does make sense to apply to corpuscles, unobservable entities, in science. Then, Putnam's first example, which I have labeled (A.), above, is correct. Trouble arises in regard to (B.), however, for how can Putnam be sure that *satellite* is a theoretical term? His explanation is this (in the sentence immediately preceding (B), quoted above: (B.*) "A theoretical term, properly so-called, is one which comes from a scientific *theory* (and the almost untouched problem, in thirty years of writing about 'theoretical terms' is what is *really* distinctive about such terms)."[64] There are several puzzling things about (B.*) and (B.); first of all, the parenthetical remark in (B*) seems to belie the statement preceding it: the preceding statement appears to tell us just what Putnam thinks is really distinctive about theoretical terms, while the parenthetical remark tells us that is not what we have just been told. How, then, are we to know whether a given term is a theoretical term at all? After all, even assuming the quoted claim (B.*) to be true, a scientific theory might adopt an observation term and apply it to an observable thing. This Putnam himself recognizes; he writes: (D.) "A scientific theory, properly so-called, may refer only to observables. (Darwin's theory of evolution, as originally put forward, is one example.)"[65]

We might consider the concept "fitness" as in "survival of the fittest" or "selection" as in "natural selection" as examples. These appear to be observation terms applied to observable entities in a scientific theory. But now there is a problem; for once we abandon the simple (if absurd) criterion for theoretical terms that they can, in principle, only be used to refer to unobservable things, it is hard to see what criterion to put in its place. How can we now tell whether *fitness* is an observation term or a theoretical term? The mere fact that it, or *satellite* occurs in a scientific theory does not by itself tell us whether it is a theoretical term. Even if we grant that a theoretical term is one

64. Putnam, "What Theories Are Not," 219.
65. Ibid., 217.

that *comes* from a scientific theory, we cannot assume *satellite,* for example, is a theoretical term merely because it fulfills that condition. (Kepler introduced the term into Latin, and astronomy, too, as the *Oxford English Dictionary* entry indicates.) For Putnam claims a scientific theory may have a vocabulary consisting entirely of observation terms, as his evolution example illustrates. So coming from a scientific theory is not a sufficient condition of a term's being a theoretical term. Is this condition even necessary? *Mass, force, energy* would seem to be counterexamples, since they surely are theoretical terms, but they do not appear to have come originally from scientific theories. (Ultimately, we need to know more about what Putnam means by "coming from a scientific theory" — after all, the word *satellite* existed in French and English prior to Kepler's introduction of it into science.)

Putnam himself seems to get confused about whether he means to claim that *satellite* is a theoretical or observational term in his footnote to (B.) There, he seems to have slipped into supposing that he is defending the claim that *satellite* is an *observation* term against objections Carnap might raise. But, of course, he has claimed it is a theoretical term though one that refers to an observable entity. Certainly, there is no reason to demand a priori that a term signify either an observation term or a theoretical term, but not both. It is Putnam who requires this, it seems, as comes out in his discussion of (C.) There, *electron* and *positron* are evidently supposed to be theoretical terms, which are nevertheless said to signify things observed. Putnam thinks of this example as an objection to the observational/theoretical distinction as traditionally made. He writes:

> This objection is sometimes dealt with by proposing to "relativize" the observation-theoretical dichotomy to the context. (Carnap, however, rejects this way out in the article we have been citing [i.e., "The Methodological Character of Theoretical Concepts"; Putnam seems to be thinking of the first paragraph on p. 49 of Carnap's paper]). This proposal to "relativize" the dichotomy does not seem to me very helpful. In the first place, one can easily imagine a context in which "electron" would occur, in the same text, in *both* observational reports and in theoretical conclusions from those reports. (So that one would have distortions if one tried

to put the term in either the "observational term" box or in the "theoretical term" box.)[66]

Apparently Putnam here feels obliged to put *electron* in one box or the other, but not in both. Yet if an observation term can refer to unobservables, there ought to be no need for this dichotomy. The dichotomy must be maintained only if we think an observation term is one which, in principle, can be used only to refer to observable things. But Putnam has already asserted that, on that condition, there are no observation terms. It is incomprehensible that he would feel the need to avoid allowing the term to rest in both boxes, unless he had slipped back into thinking of an observation term as one that can, in principle, be used only to refer to observable things. If it is granted that a supposed observation term can also refer to an unobservable entity and that a scientific theory can refer only to observables, it is hard to see what prevents the supposed observation term from *being* a theoretical term as well — especially if we suppose, as Putnam does, that a theoretical term is merely one that comes from a scientific theory.

In fairness to Putnam, it should be noted that he completes the last quoted passage with the sentence: "In the second place, for what philosophical problem or point does one require even the relativized dichotomy?"[67] This might seem to suggest that Putnam really doubts there is any dichotomy at all. The trouble with this interpretation is that he continues to use the dichotomy right down to the end of the paper. I should say here that although the view I have sketched above is one that involves relativizing the dichotomy between observational and theoretical terms, it is not to the context that I propose relativizing it (or not merely to the context); rather, it is to the technique by which the statement including the term in question is verified. Then there is no reason to demand that a term fall into one box or the other, but not both. There is no need to characterize any term as in itself either observational or theoretical, or even to insist that in one and the same context, a term be observa-

66. Ibid., 219–20.
67. Ibid., 220.

tional or theoretical, but not both. My point can be put by saying that whereas Hempel proposes to relativize this distinction but fails to do so, Putnam, who provides excellent reasons for rejecting the distinction in its absolute form, opposes relativizing it and continues to use it. He continues to use it, labeling some terms observation terms, some reports observation reports, without any explanation of the criterion by which these labels are affixed. He is content to argue merely that an observation report cannot be identified by the presence in of observation terms — as if the class of observation terms were well defined. Putnam never discusses how the distinction between observation and theoretical statements can or should be made, though he twice asserts the need for some such notion as observation report.[68]

Now Putnam is very critical of the attempt to define the dichotomy between observational and theoretical with regard to statements merely in terms of the vocabulary the statements contain. But it seems that he does not question the validity of that dichotomy with regard to terms or the validity of the dichotomy between observable and unobservable entities and properties. Indeed, he continues to use these distinctions as if they were essential ones (that is, as if there were terms that are in themselves observational and others in themselves theoretical), though these contrasts now lack any visible means of support. Whereas I claim that no term is intrinsically observational or theoretical, Putnam seems inconsistent on this point. It seems as though, for Putnam, the distinction between observable and unobservable is, in a way, just as absolute as it is for Hempel, since a term such as *red* or *hard* remains an observation term even when it is applied to an unobservable entity. The puzzle is, why doesn't it seem more paradoxical to Putnam than it evidently does to continue to refer to *red* as an observation term even when it is applied to an unobservable entity? It is hard to avoid the conclusion that he is using the term in an ontological way.

I wish to say of terms such as *repression* and *the unconscious* that although they normally signify unobservable processes and objects,

68. Ibid., 216, 220.

these terms become signifiers of observables or are able to become such. Unobservables are capable of becoming observable. Neither Putnam nor Achinstein has considered this possibility, it seems. I claim that it is precisely because of their theory-laden character that such terms are able to become designators of observables. The successful theory is the one that makes this transition possible. (The number of theories in which terms such as *the unconscious* are and remain designators of unobservables is legion; consider Schopenhauer's and Herbart's, for example.) Of course this suggestion, concerning the possibility of some terms making a transition from theoretical status to observational status, even if valid, would not guarantee that *repression* and *the unconscious* are such terms. At most what has been achieved here is the demolition of certain objections to the possibility of psychoanalysis having scientific status, that is, Wittgenstein's conventionalistic view of interpretations, James's claim that unconscious ideas are incoherent and unnecessary, and MacIntyre's concern about the unverifiability of interpretations and the unobservability of the unconscious. None has stood up very well. On the other hand, I have not proved that psychoanalysis is a science, is part of a science, or is even a scientific discipline or technology. But saying this is hardly to concede anything at all; for to prove any of these things, a definition of science would be needed, and I am not alone among philosophers in recognizing the lack of any such thing.

For Freud, what is resisted is, essentially, unconscious ideas and wishes, and this basic psychoanalytic concept can be expected to place considerable constraints on the means whereby we are going to be able to ascertain *which* ideas and wishes are resisted in any given case. What is the appropriate way to inquire into unconscious ideas and wishes in explaining resistance phenomena? For Freud, the technique that thrust itself upon him involved free association, preeminently in a clinical context. As I discussed in chapter 2, one strategy for inquiring into the appropriateness of this technique is to consider the consequences of avoiding the assumption that it is the appropriate method. Fortunately, we need not actually perform such a thought experiment, since the rejection of that assumption has already been argued for, at book length, by Adolf Grünbaum, and it is an examination of his critique of the psychoanalytic method of inquiry that comprises chapter 4.

4

. . . .

Is Psychoanalysis a Scientific Advance?
Grünbaum's Critique

By far the most important philosophical rejection of the scientific credibility of Freud's work ever to appear is Adolf Grünbaum's *The Foundations of Psychoanalysis: A Philosophical Critique*. In this work, Grünbaum examines the conception of *causality* in psychoanalytic explanations; Freud's claims to have discovered etiologies for the various psychopathologies, as well as causal explanations of dreams, parapraxes, and the effects of psychoanalytic treatment itself, are reviewed, examined, and mainly dismissed. Grünbaum does not claim that the notion of unconscious mental processes is self-contradictory, nor is it his view that psychoanalytic theories are untestable. Rather, Grünbaum maintains that it is the clinical method, relying as it does on free association to support the ascription of unconscious mental states, that is flawed and must be replaced by extraclinical testing of psychoanalytic hypotheses, that is, by tests in which longitudinal studies subject to experimental controls are employed.

To see the difficulty with such a proposal, psychoanalysis might be thought of as treating the resistances and transferences to be found clinically, that is, in free association, as the basis of "correspondence rules" (as discussed in chapter 3) for ascribing ("unobservable") unconscious ideas and wishes.[1] Then, the rejection of clinical testing in favor of extraclinical testing raises problems on two fronts: (1) when resistances and transferences in free association are no longer treated as providing any evidence at all for ascriptions of unconscious ideas and wishes, do the hypotheses that are still formulated in terms of unconscious ideas and wishes remain psychoanalytic hypotheses? and (2) more generally, how are unconscious ideas and wishes to be operationally defined, if resistance and transference phenomena in free association are no longer treated as having any role in defining them? That is, in the absence of extraclinical phenomena that can *replace* the rejected clinical data, psychoanalytic hypotheses will have been rendered effectively untestable, it seems.[2] I shall try to show that Grünbaum fails to address these problems satisfactorily; indeed, he does not address the second problem at all. One theme of this chapter will be that Grünbaum's book is a great misreading of Freud; but just as important as its numerous errors of interpretation are its pervasive logical and epistemological flaws which subvert the argument they underlie.

The book begins with a ninety-four-page introduction in which hermeneutic approaches to psychoanalysis are examined and rejected. Such approaches share the view that human action is not subject to scientific explanation because the ultimate test of whether explanations of human action are correct depends upon the self-understanding, insight, or introspection of the subject. When applied to explanations that refer to unconscious motivation, this view leads to Habermas's "cognitive enthronement of the patient" (31), according to Grünbaum.[3] In combating the hermeneutic approach,

1. I have criticized aspects of this way of thinking about psychoanalytic interpretation in chapter 3; however, employed hypothetically, it provides a convenient way of highlighting the main problems in Grünbaum's book.

2. It is important to remain clear about the radicalness of Grünbaum's rejection of clinical testing and the data it yields. He does not seek merely to *supplement* clinical testing with extraclinical testing; such a proposal would raise few problems. On the integration of psychoanalysis and experimental psychology, see M. H. Erdelyi's *Psychoanalysis: Freud's Cognitive Psychology*.

3. Unprefixed page references are to Grünbaum, *Foundations of Psychoanalysis*.

Grünbaum insists that psychoanalytic hypotheses must be testable outside the clinical situation — that is, beyond that context where patients' words have the authority Grünbaum thinks hermeneutic accounts ascribe to them. Indeed, intraclinical testing of *any* psychoanalytic interpretation is impossible because, Grünbaum assumes, employing "the *intra*clinical devices of psychoanalytic investigation" involves forsaking "the methodological safeguards of prospective causal inquiry" (170), that is, abandoning "the burdens of prospective longitudinal studies employing (experimental) controls" (141).

Nevertheless, although it is certainly true that psychoanalytic investigation pretty much excludes *experimental* prospective causal inquiry, Grünbaum's assumption is unfounded, unless one also assumes (and there is no reason to) that all prospective causal inquiry is experimental. Against this additional assumption is the fact that research on earthquakes, sunspots, and stellar nebulae, for example, is often prospective causal inquiry, yet little or none of it is experimental so far. Besides, because of ethical limits, it is hard to see what extraclinical controlled experiments could be proposed in which psychic trauma, for example, could be investigated. Grünbaum's assumption amounts to excluding from psychoanalysis, from what is "intraclinical" in it, all systematic reflection about, and action on the results of, the cathartic method or free association — for example, all making and testing of hypotheses — of the sort Freud practiced. At the very least, these include predictions to be made and acted upon concerning what interpretations particular patients will assent to or even consider, and hypotheses to be formulated concerning when and why they do so. Nor will any possible new clinical technique escape Grünbaum's demand. Such a result ought to make us realize the extreme artificiality of Grünbaum's distinction between intra- and extraclinical methods — for he appears to have no criterion for distinguishing the two — and to wonder whether some overlap of the two, or some realm between them, might not exist. In short, Grünbaum's assumption enshrines a false dichotomy between the intraclinical and the extraclinical, and a false dichotomy between the cognitive enthronement of the patient on the one hand and the canons of controlled experimentation on the other. Demanding extraclinical testing of psychoanalytic hypotheses and rejecting all evidence derived intraclinically might just possibly be comparable to demanding that all astronomical hypotheses be confirmed entirely without reliance on telescopes.

DOES THERAPEUTIC SUCCESS ONLY RESULT FROM CORRECT INTERPRETATIONS?

The second chapter of part 1, "Did Freud Vindicate His Method of Clinical Investigation?" brings us nearer to the heart of Grünbaum's book, for in it he confronts Freud on what he takes to be his own terms — namely as a scientist seeking causal explanations of pathological phenomena. Although Grünbaum accords Freud some credit for the attempt, psychoanalysis cannot in the end vindicate its claims to have accomplished what it sought, in his view, since its clinical methods and the evidence they generate are tainted. The trouble lies in Freud's supposed reliance upon what Grünbaum calls the Tally Argument. According to this argument, only interpretations that tally with what is real in the patient will be therapeutically successful; essential to that argument, for Grünbaum, is the Necessary Condition Thesis (NCT), which he formulates as follows: "(1) only the psychoanalytic method of interpretation and treatment can yield or mediate to the patient correct insight into the unconscious pathogens of his psychoneurosis, and (2) the analysand's correct insight into the etiology of his affliction and into the unconscious dynamics of his character is, in turn, *causally necessary* for the therapeutic conquest of his neurosis" (139–40). The importance of the NCT can hardly be overestimated, since, according to Grünbaum, given a positive therapeutic outcome, it provides the basis for (among other things) Freud's rejection of the claim that clinical data are contaminated by suggestion, his inference of specific sexual etiologies for the psychoneuroses by retrospective (that is, nonexperimental) methods alone, and the credence psychoanalysis gives to patients' "introspective self-observations" once their motivations "are no longer distorted or hidden by repressed conflicts" (127–28, 167).

Yet Grünbaum is able to muster only two passages in which he thinks this argument, with its NCT, is explicitly stated in Freud's writings. The main one is the following (which Grünbaum quotes on 138), in which Freud is trying to answer the objection that "the influencing of our patient [through suggestion] may make the objective certainty of our findings doubtful."[4] To this Freud replies:

> Our opponents . . . think we have 'talked' the patients into everything relating to the importance of sexual experiences — or even into those experiences themselves. . . . These accusations are contradicted more easily by an appeal to experience than by the help of theory. Anyone who has himself carried out psycho-analyses will have been able to convince himself on countless occasions that it is impossible to make suggestions to a patient in that way. The doctor has no difficulty, of course, in making him a supporter of some particular theory and in making him share some possible error of his own. In this respect the patient is behaving like anyone — like a pupil — but this only affects his intelligence, not his illness. After all, his conflicts will only be successfully solved and his resistances overcome if the anticipatory ideas he is given tally with what is real in him. Whatever in the doctor's conjectures is inaccurate drops out in the course of the analysis.[5]

It is doubtful, however, whether the NCT captures what Freud says here; first, absent from Freud's text is anything corresponding to Grünbaum's reference to conditions of *cure,* or "therapeutic conquest of . . . neurosis." Then, whereas Freud counters criticism of the "anticipatory ideas," "conjectures" supplied by the analyst, Grünbaum is concerned with the analyst's "method of interpretation," "correct insight." But Freud cannot be assumed to be using these terms synonymously. This becomes clear when other passages in which Freud uses "anticipatory idea(s)" are examined.[6] There are only twelve such passages, seven of which use the expression to refer to a general tendency of the mind to falsify perceptions in order to

---

4. Freud, *Introductory Lectures on Psycho-Analysis,* 16:452.
5. Ibid.
6. For a complete list of these passages see Guttman, *Concordance,* 1:294.

render them intelligible,[7] and, more relevantly, five use it to mean, roughly, a preliminary interpretive remark made by an analyst,[8] where a contrast with other interpretive remarks assumed to have epistemic superiority is implied.

The NCT interpretation of the passage becomes even more questionable when we note the absence in it of anything corresponding to Grünbaum's claim that Freud requires "correct insight into the etiology of his affliction" on the part of the patient as a causally necessary condition of cure. But the analyst's anticipatory ideas might tally with what is real in the patient without the patient necessarily knowing they do; does Grünbaum think Freud required that the patient not only recall repressed childhood experiences but also understand that they are the causes of his illness and how they caused it — that is, know "the unconscious dynamics of his character" — in order for therapy to succeed? Is it even obvious that Freud thought *the analyst* has to know these things for successful therapy? Only a few pages past the passage Grünbaum quotes, Freud seems to be denying it; referring to the crucial role of the transference, and of its analysis, in therapy, Freud writes:

> The decisive part of the work is achieved by creating in the patient's relation to the doctor — in the 'transference' — new editions of the old conflicts. . . . In place of his patient's true illness there appears the artificially constructed transference illness . . . we can draw no direct conclusion from the distribution of the libido during and resulting from the treatment as to how it was distributed during the illness. Not until after the transference has once more been resolved can we reconstruct in our thoughts the distribution of libido which had prevailed during the illness.[9]

A simpler interpretation of the passage Grünbaum provides to show

---

7. Freud, *Interpretation of Dreams,* 5:575, 666; *Psychopathology of Everyday Life,* 6:56, 60; "Dynamics of Transference," 12:100, 169; *On the History of the Psycho-Analytic Movement,* 14:16.

8. Freud, "Analysis of a Phobia in a Five-Year-Old Boy," 10:104; "Future Prospects of Psycho-Analytic Therapy," 11:142; *Introductory Lectures on Psycho-Analysis,* 16:437, 438, 452.

9. Freud, *Introductory Lectures on Psycho-Analysis,* 16:454–56; cf. ibid., 444–45.

Freud's supposed acceptance of the NCT is possible; Freud seems to be thinking there mainly of sexual experiences and their importance, especially childhood experiences. Then, the fact that the patient's resistance to their recall is overcome and his conflict over their importance is solved is evidence that they were not suggested to the patient by the analyst. So therapeutic success is not referred to in the passage Grünbaum supplies to show Freud formulating the Tally Argument; after all, there is more to successful therapy than recalling childhood sexual experiences and recognizing their importance. Freud's argument is essentially an appeal to experience, as he says there; try and see if it is possible, by psychoanalytic means, to suggest such specific memories to patients (Freud does not deny here the possibility of suggesting such experiences by nonpsychoanalytic means). Regardless of what one may think of Freud's appeal to experience here, the NCT seems far from his mind.

Support for this alternative to Grünbaum's interpretation of the Tally Argument text can be found in an earlier passage that is so similar as to suggest that the Tally Argument passage is Freud's own later paraphrase of it.[10] In this earlier passage, Freud explicitly separates the question of whether infantile sexual scenes reported by patients are genuine from appraisal of the results of psychoanalysis and says he will deal only with the former. Responding to the possibility that the doctor influences the patient "by suggestion to imagine and reproduce them [infantile sexual scenes]," Freud appeals to experience; he writes: "I have never yet succeeded in forcing on a patient a scene I was expecting to find, in such a way that he seemed to be living through it with all the appropriate feelings."[11] This passage supports the interpretation of the Tally Argument text according to which (a) therapeutic success is not at issue in the Tally Argument passage — the issue instead is the genuineness of certain remembered childhood sexual experiences; and (b) the argument in the Tally Argument passage occurs, not in the sentence Grünbaum focuses on, but rather in the preceding appeal to experience in therapy.

The other text Grünbaum supplies (139) to justify attributing the

10. Freud, "Aetiology of Hysteria," 3:204–6.
11. Ibid., 205.

NCT to Freud is equally troublesome; it is another passage in which Freud refers to anticipatory ideas rather than interpretations:

> In a psycho-analysis the physician always gives his patient (sometimes to a greater and sometimes to a lesser extent) the conscious anticipatory ideas by the help of which he is put in a position to recognize and to grasp the unconscious material. For there are some patients who need more of such assistance and some who need less; but there are none who get through without some of it. Slight disorders may perhaps be brought to an end by the subject's unaided efforts, but never a neurosis—a thing which has set itself up against the ego as an element alien to it. To get the better of such an element another person must be brought in, and in so far as that other person can be of assistance the neurosis will be curable.[12]

Therapeutic success is definitely the issue here—but is Freud saying that psychoanalytic treatment *alone* can provide it? What makes this so implausible is that Freud knew very well of at least one person of whom this was not true, namely himself. In his correspondence with Wilhelm Fliess, Freud refers to his own neurosis. But Freud was never in psychoanalytic treatment. To be sure, another person was "brought in," namely Fliess, but he did not analyze Freud, though perhaps it could be said that he gave some of the "conscious anticipatory ideas" Freud needed for his self-analysis.[13] Even more subversive of the NCT as a paraphrase of this text is the fact that it was drawn from Freud's case history of Little Hans (as Grünbaum notes, 139), and it was in reference to Little Hans that the words quoted above were written. But the patient was only five years old at the end of the treatment administered by his father; is it plausible that Freud would assume the second conjunct of the NCT to be true of Hans, that Hans must have achieved "correct insight into the etiology of his affliction and into the unconscious dynamics of his character" in order for therapeutic success to have resulted? Is the NCT even con-

---

12. Freud, "Analysis of a Phobia in a Five-Year-Old Boy," 10:104.

13. Freud's neurosis, and his relation to Fliess, are discussed in Jones, *Life and Work of Sigmund Freud*, 1:304–6. For the letters, see *Complete Letters of Sigmund Freud to Wilhelm Fliess*. All of Freud's references to his own neuroses can be found in the index on p. 501 under "Neuroses, Freud's."

sistent with Freud's remarking, "With Hans's last phantasy the anxiety which arose from his castration complex was also overcome"?[14] Does a five-year-old's fantasy (the "plumber" fantasy recorded by Freud two pages earlier) count as "correct insight into the etiology of his affliction and into the unconscious dynamics of his character"? There is no doubt that Freud regarded the analysis as successful.[15]

One last piece of evidence against the NCT as an account of Freud's views is the fact that the NCT does not allow for the spontaneous remission of psychoneuroses (as Grünbaum claims, 140), a claim contradicted by Freud's assertion that "the barrier erected by repression can fall before the onslaught of a violent emotional excitement produced by a real cause; it is possible for a neurosis to be overcome by reality."[16] A full discussion of the texts in which Grünbaum claims to see the NCT implicitly at work (see his references, e.g., 153, 163) would be needed to settle whether the NCT or the Tally Argument are really involved in any of them. It would be paradoxical to apologize for not dealing with these texts in detail, however; Grünbaum attributes to Freud a central thesis, on the basis of which all of Freud's work is supposed to be flawed. But Freud only asserted this thesis in two places, he claims, although neither of them seems to support the attribution very well. Granted, the NCT sounds like the sort of thing many intelligent people suppose Freud to have meant, and possibly texts can be found in which he says things close to it. But if so much is to hinge on Freud's adherence to such a thesis, ought we not be supplied with a very high order of proof that Freud did actually adhere to it? Why did he never (or hardly ever) assert it,

14. Freud, "Analysis of a Phobia in a Five-Year-Old Boy," 10:100.
15. Ibid.; see also Freud's postscript written in 1922, 10:148–49.
16. Freud, "Fragment of an Analysis of a Case of Hysteria," 7:110; see also ibid., 7:79 and "'Civilized' Sexual Morality," 9:195. Grünbaum claims that Freud ultimately accepted the existence of spontaneous remissions, but this involved abandoning the NCT; he assumes this was a late development in Freud's thought (160, 172), but the above quote refutes this assertion, since it dates from 1901 (1905 at the latest). By contrast, I claim that Freud never espoused the NCT, and thus saw no problem in recognizing the phenomenon of spontaneous remission to start with.

if it plays so central a role in his thought? Could it have played so central a role in his thought without his knowing it? What kind of verification should we require for attributing such thoughts to a person — thoughts which guide all their other thoughts, but which they are themselves unaware of holding? How are such attributions epistemically superior to the sort of interpretation Grünbaum objects to when practiced by Freud? Could the motive for attributing the NCT to Freud with so heavy a burden of significance be simply that the NCT is so eminently refutable?

But even if we grant, for the sake of argument, that Freud did hold the NCT or something like it, how central a role did it play in his thought? Does anything very much hinge on his holding it? Grünbaum thinks plenty does — for example, Freud's rejection of the claim that his clinical data are contaminated by suggestion rests on the NCT. But the quote from Freud shows him offering very different reasons; therapeutic success seems far from his mind. What about Freud's claims to have discovered specific etiologies for the psychoneuroses; was he tacitly (or overtly) relying on the NCT there? Grünbaum ignores aspects of Freud's thought for which abundant evidence exists — in particular, Freud's reliance on analogical thinking in causal inquiry.

Thus, it is the comparison of (i) hysteria provoked by accident, (ii) hysterical attacks in which the subject hallucinates the same event that provoked the first one, (iii) hysteria whose symptoms are "ostensibly spontaneous," (iv) hysterical symptoms standing in a "symbolic relation" to their precipitating cause, and (v) the typical hysterical symptoms, which led Breuer and Freud to "establish an analogy" and to claim that a "psychical trauma" is the operative cause in all.[17] The operative psychical trauma, unavailable to the patient's normal memory, is "in his memory when he is hypnotized," since "hypnosis is an artificial hysteria." Then, what was found true of hysterical symptoms "can be applied almost completely to hysterical *attacks*."[18] Again, melancholia must be compared with normal mourning for its

17. Freud, *Studies on Hysteria*, 2:4–6.
18. Ibid., 12, 13.

elucidation, and dreams serve as "the prototype in normal life of narcissistic mental disorders."[19] One analogy, appearing on the page after the one on which Grünbaum thinks the Tally Argument appears,[20] explains why suggestion is not a great hazard in interpretation, and also why the credence given to the findings of analysis is justified; the NCT is nowhere in sight. Instead, the reason for both is the coincidence between the translations of symbols and fantasies produced spontaneously by paranoids (who Freud says are above suspicion of being influenced by suggestion) and the results of analytic investigations into the unconscious of transference neurotics.[21] As before, therapeutic success has nothing to do with justifying these beliefs, for Freud. Paranoia provides the clearest evidence of this, since Freud certainly had plenty to say concerning its etiology. For Freud, the paranoid's delusions are analogous to the philosopher's internally based system-building;[22] but paranoia is not only analytically incurable, he claims, it is not even analytically treatable.[23] Grünbaum's attempt to reconcile these views of Freud's (concerning the etiology and untreatability of paranoia) with attribution of the Tally Argument to him (see 141) is obscure, too brief, and ignores the variety of data Freud actually provided, for example, in "A Case of Paranoia Running Counter to the Psycho-Analytic Theory of the Disease," in which a woman apparently suffering from delusions of being persecuted by a young *man* turns out on further inquiry to fulfill the psychoanalytic theory of paranoia as based on repressed homosexuality; her "*original* persecutor" was a woman, after all.[24]

19. Freud, "Mourning and Melancholia," 14:243.

20. Freud, *Introductory Lectures on Psycho-Analysis*, 16:453.

21. Ibid. I take Freud here to mean, not that paranoids cannot be hypnotized, for example, but rather that their "translations" arise prior to, and independent of, therapeutic intervention. In "Further Remarks on the Neuro-Psychoses of Defence" (3:177–78), Freud reports hypnotizing a paranoid patient.

22. Freud, *Totem and Taboo*, 13:73; "On Narcissism," 14:96–97; "From the History of an Infantile Neurosis," 17:61.

23. Freud, "Dynamics of Transference," 12:107; "Some Neurotic Mechanisms," 18:225.

24. Freud, "A Case of Paranoia," 14:263–72.

No therapeutic effect was even sought here, since the subject was not in treatment but was examined by Freud for purely legal purposes. Whether such data prove the truth of Freud's etiological hypotheses is not at issue; the point is that he clearly held these data to be relevant evidence,[25] which undermines the attribution of the argument Grünbaum ascribes to him.

A more just estimation of the role therapeutic success played in generating and confirming etiological hypotheses for Freud would seem to be that he thought of it as evidence, one kind of evidence, but by no means the only kind relevant and available; and although not all such analogies as the ones mentioned above offer confirmatory evidence, they are all valuable heuristic devices for Freud. I shall not argue their role as proof here, since I am not trying to show that Freud was right to infer etiologies in the ways that he did or that his results were correct, but merely that Grünbaum's model of Freud's inferences is flawed; he does not seem to realize they are analogies at all.[26] Focusing on therapeutic success as Grünbaum does has the further effect of excluding as evidence the resistances and transferences that, for Freud, were basic to his inquiry.

ARE INTERPRETATIONS CORRECT ONLY IF THERAPEUTIC SUCCESS RESULTS FROM THEM?

To move to discussing the sorts of evidence Grünbaum ignores, however, is to turn away from a glaring logical flaw in what he provides — that is, his conversion of the NCT to a very different proposition, indeed, without any argument or support for doing so at all. Here are Grünbaum's words immediately following his quote concerning the Tally Argument (*Introductory Lectures on Psycho-Analysis,* 16:452):

> Note at once that Freud acknowledges the patient's *intellectual* docility. But he emphasizes that while the doctor therefore "has no difficulty, of

25. Ibid., 266.
26. It is not a defect for scientific inquiry to rest on analogical thinking; see, for example, in Darwin's case, S. J. Gould's "Darwin's Untimely Burial."

course in making him . . . share some possible error of his own . . . this only affects his intelligence, not his illness." Thus, Freud is clearly relying on the alleged refractoriness of the neurosis to dislodgment by the mere pseudoinsights generated by incorrect conjectures on the part of the analyst. And he depends on that purported refractoriness to serve as nothing less than the epistemic underwriter of the clinical validation of his entire theory. (138)

Now the refractoriness in question is very much less than "the epistemic underwriter" of psychoanalysis, for Freud, and nothing has been said to show otherwise, even if we grant that Freud accepted the Tally Argument with its NCT. Let us assume that Grünbaum would not say of one thing that it is *the* epistemic underwriter of some truth if he thought that another equally cogent epistemic underwriter for it existed. So Grünbaum has moved from the Tally Argument's second conjunct, which I shall paraphrase as

(A) Therapeutic success results only if true interpretations have been offered (q only if p).

to

(B) True interpretations have been offered only if therapeutic success results (p only if q).

Now (A) and (B) are not equivalent, nor does either imply the other. (A) says that true interpretations are causally necessary for therapeutic success; (B) says that the only indication of an interpretation's truth is therapeutic success. According to (A), if an interpretation cures, it must be true; but an interpretation might be true even if it does not produce a cure. (B) does *not* say that if an interpretation cures, it must be true. (B) says that if an interpretation does not cure, it cannot be true.

I say that Grünbaum has *converted* (A) to (B) because no argument is offered there, nor is there even any sign that he thinks an argument might be needed, for the claim I have paraphrased as (B). Furthermore, ascriptions to Freud of statements implying (B) can be found throughout the rest of the chapter; thus Grünbaum writes:

The attribution of *therapeutic* efficacy to the lifting of repressions was indeed the epistemic basis for endowing Freud's method of free associations with the ability to certify causes (e.g., pathogens). (146)

The *empirical tenability* of this cardinal premise [the NCT] of his Tally Argument is the pivot on which he rested his generic tribute to the probative value of the clinical data obtained by the psychoanalytic method of inquiry. (148)

. . . NCT is the pivot that gave any therapeutic triumphs achieved by analysis the leverage to vouch for the authenticity of its clinical data. (159)

. . . Freud's essential reliance on positive therapeutic outcome to vindicate the probity of clinical data via NCT in the face of suggestibility is being widely overlooked. (167)

Yet not only does the chapter provide no text in which Freud is supposed to have asserted (B), or converted (A) and (B), except for the Tally Argument text itself, and Grünbaum shows no awareness that such a text should be provided; but even when faced with direct contradiction by Freud, he sweeps it aside in an apparently unwitting manner.

Thus, Grünbaum notes the fact that, for Freud, paranoia and other "narcissistic neuroses"—as distinct from the "transference neuroses"—are refractory to psychoanalysis. Grünbaum writes:

Hence in the case of the former subclass of disorders, the Tally Argument is, of course, unavailable to authenticate his clinically inferred etiologies by means of therapeutic success. Yet, in another lecture (number 27), he explicitly gave the same epistemic sanction to the clinical etiologies of the two subclasses of psychoneuroses (*S.E.* 1917, 16:438–439). And presumably he did so by *extrapolating* the therapeutic vindication of the psychoanalytic method of etiologic investigation from the transference neuroses to the narcissistic ones. (141)

As exegesis of the text cited, the last two sentences quoted are, to say the least, very muddled. What is supposed to count as "giving the same epistemic sanction to the clinical etiologies of the two subclasses of psychoneuroses' is a mystery, since Freud concludes the paragraph referred to by saying: "We are faced here by a fact [the assumed untreatability of the narcissistic neuroses] which we do not understand and which therefore leads us to doubt whether we have already understood all the determinants of our possible success with the other [i.e., the transference] neuroses." The natural interpretation is that Freud gave *superior* epistemic sanction to the etiologies of transference neuroses in comparison with those of narcissistic neuroses; for the etiology of the latter includes a determinant he *knows* he does not understand, whereas (and for that reason alone) he merely *doubts* whether he *really* understands *all* the determinants of the etiology of the former. Earlier he had thought all the determinants of the former were understood. For Freud, *parts* of the two etiologies are the same; and these parts are ascertained in the same way — "we make use of the same procedure," he says. But how can "extrapolating" from the transference neuroses to the narcissistic neuroses result in *the same* epistemic sanction for both, if ununderstood determinants are at work in the latter that are not at work in the former? And how would it be possible to "extrapolate" what is supposedly the method's only possible vindication, namely therapeutic vindication, from cases in which therapeutic vindication is taken to exist to cases in which it is not?[27]

Indeed, if anything epistemic is extrapolated in the Freud text Grünbaum cites, it seems to be *un*certainty, from the radical uncertainty concerning the etiologies of the narcissistic neuroses to the milder doubt about the etiologies of transference neuroses. It might seem that Freud is asserting that he does not understand the etiology of the narcissistic neuroses simply because he cannot treat (and cure) them, which is thus a tacit acceptance of (B); but this would be a mistake, since Freud is bothered here by the fact that he does not understand why the narcissistic neuroses are, as he thinks, untreatable — which implies that he is not assuming that the explanation (of their untreatability) would necessarily make psychoanalytic treatment of them possible. Indeed, by the end of the lecture from which Grünbaum quotes, Freud has sketched an explanation of the untreatability in question.[28]

Grünbaum's remark about extrapolation reveals his inability to

27. Grünbaum later makes this point himself (187–88), but against "misextrapolations" of the etiology for neuroses to ones for parapraxes and dreams.

28. Freud, *Introductory Lectures on Psycho-Analysis,* 16:444–47.

consider the possibility that Freud did not accept (B) and did not think (B) followed from, or was equivalent to, (A), even if we suppose that Freud did accept (A). Grünbaum does not bother even to speculate on how *else,* aside from extrapolation, Freud might have thought anything could be known about the etiology of paranoia — given that Freud also claimed paranoia was inaccessible to psychoanalytic treatment. But if one does not confuse (A) and (B), there is no difficulty in understanding how Freud could have views concerning the etiology of paranoia while believing it impossible to cure paranoia with them. For (A) merely says that a necessary condition of cure is a true interpretation; (A) does not say that if you have a true interpretation, you must be able to cure with it, which is what (B) claims. Why then does Grünbaum even feel the need to saddle Freud with a forced explanation of how therapeutic vindication might be "extrapolated" from cases in which it is supposed to exist to paranoia, where it was supposed not to exist, unless he ascribes (B) to Freud, and confuses (A) and (B) himself — that is, unless Grünbaum himself also assumes that the vindication of *any* interpretations (concerning, for example, etiologies or their determinant parts) must be based on their therapeutic success? For this assumption underlies the only extraclinical test (apart from longitudinal studies) Grünbaum proposes that he thinks might confirm a psychoanalytic hypothesis — the one for Freud's etiology for paranoia (38); apparently, he simply assumes any such confirming test would be one whose upshot would be a decrease in the incidence of paranoia — that is, therapeutic success, if the etiology is correct.

TESTING FREUD'S ETIOLOGY OF PARANOIA

Grünbaum offers two extraclinical tests of the psychoanalytic hypothesis concerning the etiology of paranoia; that is, the hypothesis that (a) "repressed homosexuality is a necessary condition of paranoia" (the "individual test," discussed below, can only disconfirm [a], as we shall see). That Freud held (a) is beyond doubt; thus he writes: "patients suffering from paranoia are struggling against an intensification of their homosexual trends . . . paranoia is determined by homosexuality . . . the delusion of persecution invariably depends on homosexuality,"[29] where he assumes the reader will fill in the key role of repression in the formula. What such remarks mean is obviously relevant to determining the truth of (a); but it is also relevant to determining whether (a) is testable extraclinically, even if (a) is regarded as false. So we are not concerned with the truth of (a), although we are concerned with what Freud thought the truth of (a) consisted in. If Grünbaum's account of what Freud meant by (a) is flawed, his reasons for asserting (b) "hypothesis (a) is testable extraclinically" are potentially flawed, too.

Grünbaum formulates the first of his two proposed tests in support of (b) as follows:

> Freud's etiology of paranoia postulates that repressed *homosexual* love is *causally necessary* for being afflicted by paranoid delusions (*S.E.* 1915, 14:265–66). And when the pathogenically required intensity of repression exists, it is largely engendered by the strong social taboo on homosexuality. Thus the detailed pathogenesis of paranoia envisioned by Freud warrants the following expectation: A significant decline in the social sanctions against this atypical sexual orientation should issue in a marked decrease in the incidence of paranoia. (38)

I shall refer to this as the *social test* of Freud's etiological hypothesis (a). Grünbaum's second test of the same hypothesis is as follows: suppose, he writes, that

> a paranoid woman now living in San Francisco as a self-declared lesbian comes to analysis because many of her social interactions are troubled. *Before having lifted any of her repressions,* her analyst may well become aware of both her openly lesbian life-style and of her pronounced paranoid delusions. . . . If the analyst who is seeing the putative lesbian in San Francisco is an orthodox Freudian, he will sit up all the more and notice the following discomfiting state of affairs: although the patient is paranoid, she clearly does not harbor the minimum of repression of homosexual desires that Freud's etiology claims to be the *sine qua non* for the pathogenesis of her delusional affliction. In short, before having begun to undo such full-blown repressions as she may harbor, her doctor will

29. Freud, "A Case of Paranoia," 14:265–66.

realize that he has on his couch an authentic refuting instance of the received etiology. (40)

Since, according to Grünbaum, it requires only one active lesbian (or male homosexual) who is paranoid to refute the psychoanalytic hypothesis (a) that repressed homosexuality is the causal sine qua non of paranoia, I'll refer to this as the *individual test* of that hypothesis. Although this second test involves observations by a practicing psychoanalyst, Grünbaum regards it as an extraclinical test, simply because the test is concluded before "repression-lifting" has taken place.[30] Both tests are illegitimate, however, for they are not really based on genuine implications of Freud's theory.

What Freud means by (a), according to Grünbaum, is really (c) "the 'pathogenically required' degree of intensity of repression on homosexuality necessary for causing paranoia is 'largely engendered by the strong social taboo on homosexuality.'" To see the problem in attributing (c) to Freud, or in trying to use (c) to test (a), as Grünbaum does, we need to consider the nature of repression as Freud outlines it in his account of paranoia and to consider whether the social taboo on homosexuality is, for Freud, the cause of the repression of homosexuality that he thinks causes paranoia. We shall see that (c) is not part of Freud's theory, nor is it even compatible with it.

According to Freud, the first phase of repression is *fixation*, in which an instinct or instinctual component is inhibited in its development and remains at an infantile stage. This is the necessary condition of every repression. The second phase is *repression proper*, which consists of "a detachment of the libido from people —

30. It needs to be assumed here, apparently, that it is possible to determine whether someone is or is not paranoid prior to any clinical endeavor. (MacIntyre makes a similar assumption, as noted above, p. 90, commenting on pp. 64–66 of his book.) A similar assumption also appears to underlie Grünbaum's social test: thus, he assumes that it is possible to discover whether the incidence of paranoia in a population has declined entirely apart from (presumably, some quite massive) clinical endeavor. For if clinical endeavor is needed to determine these things, then the tests in question are obviously not truly extraclinical.

and things — that were previously loved." The third phase is the most important for pathological phenomena; Freud says; it consists in *the return of the repressed,* which originates with the point of fixation, implying a regression of libidinal development to that point. In paranoia, the detachment of phase two is distinguished by the use made of the libido after it has been set free; whereas normally substitutes are sought for the lost attachment, in paranoia, "the liberated libido becomes attached to the ego, and is used for the aggrandizement of the ego." Thus, in paranoia, phase three consists in a "step back from sublimated homosexuality to narcissism."[31]

It is now possible to see how far removed Grünbaum's statement (c) is from anything Freud had in mind; for the social taboo on homosexuality that Grünbaum's social test refers to cannot be what largely engenders the repression of homosexuality necessary for causing paranoia in Freud's account. At most, that social taboo might accomplish repression proper, that is, the withdrawal of libido. But the taboo on homosexuality cannot determine what use the withdrawn libido will be put to — whether it will be sublimated or regress to fixation at the narcissistic stage. That is why Freud says of the withdrawal of libido that "it cannot in itself be the pathogenic factor in paranoia."[32] The repression necessary for causing paranoia does not result if the repressed libido is sublimated or regresses to some stage other than the narcissistic. Nor is there any basis for attributing narcissistic fixation to start with to the social taboo on homosexuality. So there is no reason why Freud's theory should be assumed to predict a decrease in the incidence of paranoia once the taboo on homosexuality is lifted. Indeed, if paranoiacs are "struggling against an intensification of their homosexual trends," any situation in which such trends could be gratified — for example, when social sanctions against homosexuality are lifted — might as easily be expected to increase the incidence of paranoia as decrease it, for Freud. To accept (c) as part of psychoanalytic theory we must

31. Freud, "Psycho-Analytic Notes on an Autobiographical Account," 12:67–72.
32. Ibid., 72.

identify the repression of homosexuality that is causative of paranoia with repression proper alone, an identification that Freud explicitly denied. In short, if (c) is rejected, Grünbaum's extraclinical
social test is not really a test of a psychoanalytic hypothesis at all.

Grünbaum's (c) does not merely state that the social taboo on
homosexuality causes homosexuality to be repressed; that claim is a
truism, probably a tautology. (After all, it would not even be a
taboo, if it did not produce repression.) Grünbaum claims that the
social taboo on homosexuality is mainly responsible for the repressed homosexuality that is causative of paranoia. That the social
taboo on homosexuality has a special position in causing paranoia is
not a truism or a tautology; indeed, no reason has been given for
even thinking it true, nor has any reason been given for thinking that
Freud thought it true. Nothing in Freud's theory implies (c), and
much goes against it.

What of Grünbaum's proposed extraclinical individual test of (a);
would the discovery of even one practicing homosexual who is paranoid refute Freud's theory of paranoia, as Grünbaum supposes? To
make such an inference involves commitment to a peculiar criterion
of repression of homosexual trends, namely — (d) "people repress
homosexual trends in themselves only if they are not actively homosexual." Proof of Grünbaum's commitment to (d) is that he infers
from the mere assumption that his hypothetical lesbian paranoiac
is actively homosexual that she does not repress her homosexual
trends. Grünbaum must assume (d), otherwise discovery of a paranoid but active homosexual would not subvert Freud's hypothesis
(a), as Grünbaum claims. Does Freud assume (d), even tacitly? Indirect evidence that he does not occurs in his account of the first phase
of repression, where he writes, "Fixation can be described in this
way. One instinct or instinctual component fails to accompany the
rest along the anticipated normal path of development, and in consequence of this inhibition in its development, it is left behind at
a more infantile stage."[33] For Freud, one instinctual component can
be fixated while others are not. So some homosexual components
might be fixated, and might be repressed, while others are not. It

33. Ibid., 67.

follows that active homosexuals might repress some homosexual components in themselves while not repressing others. A comment of Freud's about Schreber brings this out; concerning Schreber's fantasy of being a woman for the sexual pleasure of his psychiatrist, Flechsig, Freud writes, "The feminine phantasy, which aroused such violent opposition in the patient, thus had its root in a longing, intensified to an erotic pitch, for his father and brother."[34] Assuming that at least some active homosexuals share Schreber's incestuous wishful fantasies, and that, like Schreber's, such fantasies remain unconscious,[35] it is also safe to assume that many are never acted on. This illustrates the possibility, from a psychoanalytic viewpoint, of active homosexuals repressing some homosexual longings, while not repressing, that is acting on, others. A high degree of intensity of repression on some homosexual longings may accompany a low degree of intensity on others, in the same person at the same time. In this, homosexual longings are no different from heterosexual ones. Assumption (d) therefore fails. People might act on some of their homosexual trends while repressing others; and then the libido, if unsublimated, might be used for "the aggrandizement of the ego" — so there is no psychoanalytic reason to expect paranoia simply to vanish once a person begins to be homosexually active. Thus, the proposed individual test fails to test any genuinely psychoanalytic hypothesis about the etiology of paranoia, for a reason also defeating the proposed social test — in both, repression is seriously misunderstood.

If the sense of Freud's hypothesis (a) is retained, it is hard to see how its truth can be tested extraclinically — that is, by "prospective longitudinal studies employing (experimental) controls," as Grünbaum quite generally (141) proposes.

FREUD'S ETIOLOGY OF ANXIETY NEUROSIS

An even clearer case of Grünbaum's commitment to (B) than his handling of Freud's etiology for paranoia is his handling of

34. Ibid., 50.
35. Ibid., 45.

Freud's etiology for anxiety neurosis, with which he ends his reply to the question, "Did Freud vindicate his method of clinical investigation?" (the title of chapter 2). As Grünbaum notes, for Freud anxiety neurosis "does not originate in a repressed idea but turns out to be *not further reducible by psychological analysis, nor amenable to psychotherapy*," since it "is the product of all those factors which prevent the somatic sexual excitation from being worked over psychically."[36] Grünbaum writes: "Therefore, analytic treatment cannot remove its specific cause by means of psychoanalytic insight into the significance of its symptoms. It follows that the very etiology of anxiety neurosis that Freud had inferred by causal inquiry *a la* J. S. Mill provided theoretical reasons for concluding that this specific etiology could never have been disclosed, let alone validated, by the *intra*clinical devices of psychoanalytic investigation" (169–70). Contrasting Freud's account of anxiety neurosis (an "actual neurosis"), which he admires, with his handling of the psychoneuroses, Grünbaum goes on: "How, then, could that same Freud have forsaken the methodological safeguards of prospective causal inquiry, and have been content to employ the purely *intra*clinical psychoanalytic method to discover and validate the *infantile* etiologies of the psychoneuroses retrospectively?" (ibid.) Grünbaum's argument here seems to rest on the claim (seemingly, a quibble) that since psychoanalysis is a technique for discovering the repressed ideas causative of psychopathology, the discovery that a certain symptom does *not* rest on a repressed idea *cannot* be the result of psychoanalytic inquiry — even though the obvious way to discover this fact would be to search for some repressed idea associated with the symptom and record the absence of any such finding. This was Freud's view of the matter, and the way in which he seems to have arrived at the etiology for anxiety neurosis. The evidence for this comes from Drafts B and E (2/8/1893 and 6/6/1894?), which were sent to Fliess and in which Freud says that he first thought some cases of anxiety neurosis had "an apparently rational connection with a psychic trauma"; he continues:

36. Freud, "On the Grounds for Detaching a Particular Syndrome from Neurasthenia," 3:97, 109.

All I know about it is this: It quickly became clear to me that the anxiety of my neurotic patients had a great deal to do with sexuality; and in particular it struck me with what certainty coitus interruptus practiced on a woman leads to anxiety neurosis. Now, at first I followed various false tracks. I thought that the anxiety from which the patients suffer should be looked on as a continuation of the anxiety felt during the sex act—that is to say, that it actually was a *hysterical* symptom.[37]

Thus, although he had first written of one patient that the essential origin of her fear of people was the persecution to which she had been subjected after her husband's death, he appended the following footnote: "At the time I wrote this I was inclined to look for a *psychical* origin for all symptoms in cases of hysteria. I should now explain this sexually abstinent woman's tendency to anxiety as being due to *neurosis* (i.e., anxiety neurosis)."[38] It is easy to see what could have led Grünbaum into supposing that the etiology of anxiety neurosis was discovered and validated by Freud apart from psychoanalytic investigation—indeed, that it *could not* have been discovered or validated *by* psychoanalytic investigation—it is that once anxiety neurosis has been identified, isolated from hysteria (which Freud was the first to do), its etiology can then be stated without reference to repressed ideas. But Freud left no doubt that the very existence of such a distinct entity as anxiety neurosis occurred to him only after he had first confused it with hysterical symptoms; only then was he led to the etiology for it which he considered the result of psychoanalytic research.[39]

Grünbaum's refusal to attribute the discoverable *absence* of a repressed idea to psychoanalytic inquiry simply because psychoanalysis is supposed to discover the *presence* of repressed ideas is analogous to saying that research proving that some mysterious disease was not produced by a certain virus could not be medical research, since medical research is supposed to discover what causes disease. And the further assumption Grünbaum needs to argue as he does is,

37. Freud, *Complete Letters of Sigmund Freud to Wilhelm Fliess*, 43, 78.
38. Freud, *Studies on Hysteria*, 2:65.
39. Freud, *Three Essays on the Theory of Sexuality*, 7:224n.

once again, that the "*intra*clinical devices of psychoanalytic investigation" *exclude* Mill's methods and "the methodological safeguards of prospective causal inquiry."

These historical and interpretive points help in examining the inference Grünbaum draws in the passage quoted (169–70). We know one of Grünbaum's premises, for it is also a view of Freud's, namely, (C) "No psychoanalytic interpretation (that is, of unconscious ideas and wishes) can cure anxiety neurosis." We also know the conclusion Grünbaum wishes to draw; it is (E) "No (intraclinical) psychoanalytic method of investigation can lead to a correct interpretation of anxiety neurosis." The missing premise needed to make this argument valid would seem to be (D) "A(n intraclinical) psychoanalytic method of investigation can lead to a correct interpretation of anxiety neurosis only if the interpretation it leads to can cure anxiety neurosis." Now (D) is merely a variant of (B); once again, we seem to have arrived at that illicit inference from (A), hidden in Grünbaum's own theorizing.

THE REPRESSION ETIOLOGY OF THE PSYCHONEUROSES

Further confirmation of Grünbaum's own implicit acceptance of (B) comes at the very beginning of part 2 of his book, where Grünbaum discusses Breuer and Freud's "Preliminary Communication" of 1893, with which their *Studies on Hysteria* begins. Grünbaum examines and criticizes the reasoning they provide: "To claim therapeutic support for their etiologic identification of an original act of repression as the specific pathogen initially responsible for the formation of the neurotic symptom" (178). Because he finds their reasoning faulty, Grünbaum denies that there is any basis at all for the repression etiology of the neuroses:

> What, then, is the evidence they give for their etiologic identification of the repressed experience of a particular traumatic event E as the pathogen — avowedly *not* as the mere precipitator! — of a given symptom S that first appeared at the time of E? Plainly and emphatically, they predicate their identification of the repression of E as the pathogen of S on the fact that the abreactive lifting of that repression issued in the durable *removal*

of *S*. And, as their wording shows, they appreciate all too well that *without* this symptom removal, neither the mere painfulness of the event *E*, nor its temporal coincidence with *S*'s first appearance, nor yet the mere fact that the hysteric patient had repressed the trauma *E* could justify, even together, blaming the pathogenesis of *S* on the repression of *E*. (178–79)

Assuming the last quoted sentence's list (of conditions other than cure possibly relevant to proving that the repression of *E* is the pathogen of *S*) is complete, the sentence commits Grünbaum to saying that Breuer and Freud were right to hold that an interpretation is true only if it produces symptom removal, which implies (B).

It is unclear what in Breuer and Freud's *wording* is supposed to show that they appreciate what Grünbaum claims they do. Moreover, despite Grünbaum's emphatic denial, Breuer and Freud are discussing the relation between the *precipitating* cause — that is, the psychical trauma — and the hysterical symptom in the passage he quotes.[40] Indeed, that is all that is discussed in the entire first section of the "Preliminary Communication," which is all that Grünbaum is concerned with here. The "specific cause" of any symptom, or of hysteria itself, is not discussed at all in the "Preliminary Communication," as its last paragraph makes clear; indeed, the expression *specific cause* is totally absent, whereas the phrase *precipitating event/factor/cause* occurs repeatedly. Certainly, Freud means to find a "path from the symptoms of hysteria to its aetiology"[41] by induction, so this passage is not irrelevant; but its relevance is not what Grünbaum takes it to be.

At least as important as Grünbaum's tacit commitment to (B) is something he seems unaware of, though it is evident in both of the texts from Freud[42] that Grünbaum supplies to prove his point:

> [E]ach individual hysterical symptom immediately and permanently disappeared when we had succeeded in bringing clearly to light the memory of the event by which it was provoked and in arousing its accompanying affect [emphasis in original]. (178)

40. Freud, *Studies on Hysteria*, 2:6–7.
41. Freud, "Aetiology of Hysteria," 3:193.
42. These texts from Freud are in Freud, *Studies on Hysteria*, 2:6–7.

... the symptoms, which sprang from separate causes, were separately removed. (179)

Indeed, the unnoticed point is present when Grünbaum himself writes: "The separate symptom removals are made to carry the vital probative burden of discrediting the threatening rival hypothesis of placebo effect, wrought by mere suggestion" (179).[43] For it is not mere symptom removal that Breuer and Freud offer as evidence of the sort of causal relation they claim obtains between the memory of a psychical trauma and the hysterical symptom — it is the *separateness* of the removal that matters, the same separateness to be found in the relations between and among the symptom, the psychical trauma, and the memory and affect abreacted. More precisely, they establish the *existence* of a causal relation between psychical trauma and hysterical symptom by analogy; what the separateness of the symptoms' removal indicates is the *kind* of causal relation involved.

To see the central role played by the separateness of the symptom removal, consider the following thought-experiment. Suppose we list all the relevant possible outcomes of abreaction — that is, of recollection of the symptom's precipitating cause joined by its accompanying affect. There are four: (1) separate removal of the symptom, (2) nonseparate removal, (3) separate nonremoval, and (4) nonseparate nonremoval. Now (2) is conceivable; this can be made clear in contrast to (1) by considering any set of symptoms, for example, the following selection from those presented to Breuer by Anna O.: inability to drink, macropsia and convergent squint, spasm of the glottis, inability to speak, *tussis nervosa*.[44] Each symptom led the

43. The claim contained in this quote is mistaken, but in a manner not directly relevant to the present point. Briefly, Breuer and Freud do not offer symptom removal to discredit the rival hypothesis that what is operative in such cases is unconscious suggestion. What does discredit that hypothesis for them and supports the claim that it is "the verbal utterance [by the patient] which is the operative factor" (*Studies on Hysteria*, 2:7) in the cathartic method is the *spontaneity* of the process in the earliest case (Anna O.). Breuer's "great surprise" there is supposed to indicate that the whole thing was initiated by the patient.

44. Freud, *Studies on Hysteria*, 2:34, 39–40.

patient, when hypnotized (in Anna O.'s case, when auto-hypnotized), to recall a psychical trauma, and when the memory of that trauma and its affect were abreacted, the symptom presented was removed. This is separate removal, a necessary condition of which is that the symptom removed by abreaction of the affect attached to the psychical trauma recalled under hypnosis must be the same symptom as the one that led to the recall of the trauma in the first place.

To see the possibility of (2), nonseparate removal, imagine that the abreaction of one such memory's affect resulted in the removal, *not* of the original symptom presented (which, under hypnosis, led to the recall of that memory), but rather to the removal of some other symptom. In separate removal, as reported by Breuer, the patient's inability to drink led to the memory of an event that filled her with disgust — that of her lady-companion giving her dog a drink out of a glass; and her disturbances of vision led to the recall of her tearful vigil at the bedside of her dying father, when she tried to suppress her tears so that he would not see them. The abreaction of each trauma's affect led to the release of the symptom that led (under hypnosis) to the memory of the trauma.

But now suppose that the abreaction of the affect at her lady-companion's behavior led to the release, not of her inability to drink, but of her disturbances of vision, and the abreaction of the affect at her tearful vigil led to the release, not of her disturbances of vision, but of her inability to drink. Alternatively, suppose the recall and abreaction of one psychical trauma'a affect, say her suppressed tears at her father's bedside, resulted in the removal of all the other symptoms (spasm of the glottis, lost power of speech, etc.) with which it was not causally linked under hypnosis, whereas the one symptom with which it was linked under hypnosis, that is, her disturbances of vision, could only be removed in a bundle, along with the set of other symptoms, when some other psychical trauma's affect is abreacted, say, the disgust at her lady-companion's behavior.

The imaginary cases suggested here illustrate that mere symptom removal without the separateness Breuer and Freud write of would *not* support the repression hypothesis; these cases in fact would lend support to what Breuer and Freud mean by an *agent provocateur* relation between trauma and hysterical symptom, which they reject.[45] So their finding of separate removal supports the kind of causal relation Breuer and Freud claim exists between psychical trauma and hysterical symptom — namely, the symptom is a kind of reminiscence of the trauma, even though the patient does not realize it. To say this is to accept a necessary condition of Breuer and Freud's repression hypothesis — namely, that the psychical trauma which was the precipitating cause of the hysterical symptom and the symptom itself "are just as strictly related"[46] as are the accident and the symptom it provoked in traumatic hysteria (where the patient's conscious memory of the accident is unproblematic), a claim not at all obvious, to medical researchers or to patients, as is easily grasped from any of the items on the short list of symptoms Breuer and Freud give: neuralgia, tic, anorexia, disturbance of vision, and so on. If separate removal of symptoms is not found (or if separate nonremoval is not, either), it is hard to see how we could continue to say that the hysterical symptom is a *reminiscence* of the psychical trauma that is abreacted, or indeed, why we should even suppose that the "ostensibly spontaneous" hysterical symptom is due to a trauma at all. So *non*separate removal would seriously undermine the repression hypothesis — for in that case it would be hard to make out what is being repressed in hysteria, or why. Whereas with separate removal, both questions have clear answers — what is repressed is the memory (and its affect) of the psychical trauma the symptom is a reminiscence of, and the cause of the memory's repression is the impossibility or unacceptability of verbalizing the idea and discharging the affect relating to that memory.[47] The claim that "hysterical patients suffer from incompletely abreacted psychical traumas"[48] expresses more or less literally what the claims that the symptom is a

45. Ibid., 6–7.
46. Ibid., 4.
47. Freud, *Studies on Hysteria,* 2:10.
48. Freud, "On the Psychical Mechanism of Hysterical Phenomena," 3:38; cf. Freud, *Studies on Hysteria,* 2:10.

"reminiscence," or a "mnemic symbol"[49] put somewhat metaphorically. So not only is mere symptom removal by itself not the only test of an interpretation's correctness — it is not even *a* test of it. For unless the symptom removal is accomplished in a way that illustrates *separateness,* more harm than good has been done to the repression hypothesis.

This point is strengthened when we consider possibility (3), separate nonremoval. If Grünbaum were correct to attribute (B) to Freud, this ought to be an empty category. But it seems tailor-made for the narcissistic neuroses, of which Freud remarks, "[i]n them, too, it had been a question of an original conflict between the ego and the libido which led to repression — though this may call for a different topographical description; in them, too, it is possible to trace the points in the patient's life at which the repression occurred." still, "our therapeutic procedure is never successful."[50] I take this to mean that something like "separateness" is satisfied, but without therapeutic success — that is, it is a case of separate nonremoval.

Although Grünbaum is committed to (B) — that is, to the view that therapeutic success must result from an interpretation for it to be proved true — he does not regard therapeutic success as sufficient to prove it true. Thus even granting their success with the cathartic method

> would not have warranted Breuer's and Freud's *extrapolation* that the repression of *E* was also a causally necessary condition for the *origination* of *S*. For, as Morris Eagle has remarked, their therapeutic conclusion does comport with the following *contrary etiologic hypotheses*: The *conscious* traumatic experience itself as distinct from its ensuing repression — was responsible for the *initial formation of S,* whereupon the displeasure (anxiety) from the trauma actuated the repression of *E,* which is causally necessary for the mere *maintenance* of *S.* Chapter 8 will highlight the significance of this failure to offer cogent evidence for the initiating path-

49. Freud, *Studies on Hysteria,* 2:297.
50. Freud, *Introductory Lectures on Psycho-Analysis,* 16:438.

ogenic role of repression. Such evidence would be furnished by data militating *against* the rival hypothesis that repression is etiologically irrelevant to the initial formation of the symptoms. (180–81)

The contrary hypothesis Grünbaum offers raises puzzles of its own, however; it seems to require that the conscious traumatic experience cause the initial formation of the symptom (prior to repression) and apart from the displeasure presumably constitutive of it. For the displeasure of the trauma explains only the *maintenance* of the symptom once formed. But a trauma that is not unpleasurable is presumably no trauma at all. Abstracting the displeasure of a trauma from other features of it may have its uses, but it seems plainly false to make it a condition of a causal explanation of symptom formation that the trauma and its displeasure *must* occur at different times and that anything capable of being called a symptom has been formed in the total absence of displeasure. What would make E traumatic at all, if it is not unpleasurable? What aspect of the trauma other than its displeasure would initiate symptom formation prior to the displeasure that Grünbaum supposes to cause the repression? Even odder is the idea that the repression of E is necessary only for the maintenance of S. For, of course, if unmaintained, S would not exist. It is curious to offer this as a case in which repression is etiologically irrelevant — that is, one in which there would literally *be* no symptom to discuss the etiology of, if S goes unmaintained by repression. Would E be a trauma at all, and would whatever E causes be a symptom at all, unless repression ensues and "maintains" it?[51]

Further complications arise. What, for example, is there for repression to maintain, unless the symptom is a reminiscence? Indeed, why is the symptom maintained at all unless it contains something unabreacted in it? In other words, why is *repression* the mode of maintaining the symptom? Besides, Grünbaum's claim that Breuer

---

51. The "Preliminary Communication" does present an etiology for hysterical symptoms that does not involve repression, but instead involves hypnoid states. Freud told Fliess, however, that Breuer had forced the hypnoid state etiology upon him (Freud, *Complete Letters of Sigmund Freud to Wilhelm Fliess*, 411), and he quickly repudiated it.

and Freud failed to offer cogent evidence "for the initiating pathogenic role of repression" is odd (chapter 8 does not seem to offer any
help here, despite Grünbaum's promise); for one might suppose that
separateness, whether of removal or of nonremoval, counts as evidence supporting the repression hypothesis and "militating *against*
the rival hypothesis that repression is etiologically irrelevant to the
initial formation of the symptoms" (181). The rival theory Breuer
and Freud know of, Charcot's agent provocateur account, has the
feature Grünbaum refers to — repression is etiologically irrelevant —
and this theory *is* militated against by the separateness they describe.
The Grünbaum-Eagle contrary hypothesis seems empirically false,
since it requires that the displeasure of a trauma in symptom formation *not* coincide with the trauma, when it apparently often does,
and leaves unanswered more questions than it answers. Grünbaum's
objection to "the initiating pathogenic role of repression" is troubling; after all, one might suppose Breuer and Freud agree that the
psychical trauma (or the memory of it) initiated the formation of the
hysterical symptom — repression, after all, cannot occur without
something to be repressed. Unless one reads the contrary hypothesis
as merely a rewording of Breuer and Freud's theory, it is hard to see
what supports it, since it is at odds with the observed facts at a fairly
superficial level.

SLIPS: DOES FREE ASSOCIATION REVEAL CAUSES?

This claim, that repression has not been shown to have any
etiological role (even if it is granted that it occurs and that lifting
repression has therapeutic value), is also at the center of Grünbaum's
critique of Freud's account of slips. There, Grünbaum criticizes the
famous example of the young man who forgot the Latin word *aliquis* when quoting a line from Virgil's *Aeneid* ("'Let someone [*aliquis*] arise from my bones as an avenger") to express his frustration
and resentment at the widespread discrimination against Jews.[52]
Once Freud provides the forgotten word, the young man's free asso-

52. Freud, *Psychopathology of Everyday Life,* 6:9.

ciations quickly led (via *a-liquis*, fluidity, fluid, etc.) to his anxiety about his lady-friend's period, without which his fear that she was pregnant by him would be confirmed, a "contrary thought"[53] to his wish for descendants to avenge him. According to Freud, this anxious uncertainty made the young man forget the word *aliquis*. According to Grünbaum, the example illustrates the groundlessness of the method of free association in tracing causes. Grünbaum's challenge to Freud's argument is this: even granting for argument's sake that

> there is some kind of *uncontaminated causal linkage* between the restored awareness of *aliquis* . . . which triggers the labyrinthine sequence of associations, on the one hand, and the emerging anxiety thought with which the sequence terminated . . . on the other. . . . Why indeed should the *repressed* fear be held to have caused the *forgetting* of *aliquis* at the outset just because meandering associations starting out from the restored memory of *aliquis* issued in the conscious emergence of the fear? (192)

The mistaken trust in free association to reveal causes can be laid to two beliefs, according to Grünbaum. One is reliance on *post hoc ergo propter hoc* reasoning — that is, the faith that the mere fact that one thing follows another in time means that the first *caused* the second, And the second is the failure to recognize that "mere thematic affinity alone simply does not bespeak causal lineage [*sic*]" (198). When we dismiss these erroneous beliefs from our minds, free association has little appeal as a method for uncovering the causes of slips.

But should we dismiss these beliefs as errors? When the phenomena under consideration are human thought and discourse, the temporal order in which things are said and thought is surely meaningful and, very generally, causally significant. It is very difficult to conceive of a piece of human discourse, however spontaneous, in which the temporal order of the words or ideas signifies no causal connection between the earlier and the later ones; only if distracting

53. Ibid., 14.

events (not, for example, the speaker's thoughts or utterances) continually intervene is this imaginable. As for "thematic affinity," to speak of an affinity of any kind between things signifies quite generally some kind of *causal* relation between them. It would take heroic efforts of abstraction (probably unsuccessful) to listen to another person, suspending entirely our strong "bias" toward the assumption that the thematic affinities and temporal sequences in their words have a causal linkage. In the absence of any arguments from Grünbaum to support his claims, it is hard to see why we should move beyond the limits of intelligibility in order to avoid what he defines by *fiat* to be universal errors (which they often are, in other contexts).[54]

Strictly speaking, of course, Grünbaum only claimed that *mere* thematic affinity "does not bespeak causal lineage" — he did not deny that there might exist some kind of thematic affinity which would bear crucially on the causal relevance of one idea to another, as he himself wanders into conceding (by implication), when he considers in passing that the *strength* of a thematic affinity might bear upon whether that thematic affinity is causally relevant to a given effect (199). But to grant that (a) some thematic affinities are stronger than others and that (b) the degree of that strength bears upon the causal relevance of the thematic affinity in question is to open up a whole new kind of inquiry concerning causality, one not easily accommodated in the terms Grünbaum sketches in the remarks scattered throughout the book about the concept of causality. For example, he writes:

> The *causal relevance* of an antecedent state X to an occurrence Y . . . is a matter of whether X . . . MAKES A DIFFERENCE to the occurrence of Y, or AFFECTS THE INCIDENCE of Y . . . in psychology, no less than in physics and somatic medicine — *causal relevance* is a less demanding, logically weaker relation than either being causally sufficient or being causally necessary. In medicine, for example, there is evidence that heavy

54. This paragraph is loosely based on Freud's remarks in defense of the technique of free association in *Interpretation of Dreams*, 5:528–32.

tobacco smoking is indeed causally relevant to cardiovascular disease and to lung cancer. But it is a commonplace that such smoking is neither causally necessary nor causally sufficient for acquiring these illnesses. (72–73)

The main problem is that Grünbaum is much more articulate about what causal relevance is *not* than about what it is; a positive account of this concept and of why "mere thematic affinity alone simply does not bespeak causal lineage" is needed if Grünbaum's claims are to be accepted. Indeed, to grant (a) and (b) is to open up the possibility of intraclinical testing of interpretations, given standards of the strength of thematic affinities — that is, it would give free associations evidential weight bearing upon the causal relevance of one idea to another.

These results are hardly surprising. If we return to the *aliquis* example, it is pretty clear that the kind of epidemiological and experimental evidence relevant to, for example, the lung cancer case, is going to be hard to come by here. We cannot count on finding in nature even one more case similar to that one in relevant respects — a young man who (i) is worried that his girlfriend may be pregnant, (ii) is resentful of anti-semitic career obstacles, (iii) expresses his resentment by quoting a particular line of Latin verse from memory, and so on. Even more far-fetched would seem to be the idea of re-creating such a situation repeatedly, in a controlled experiment. It is no use bringing in S. Timpanaro's paleographic evidence, as Grünbaum does at this point (194–99); for we are not asking why scribes (or people in general) sometimes lose the word *aliquis* in *transcribing* the Latin text, as Timpanaro considers — we are interested in why *this* man forgot the word on *that* occasion.[55] The scribe simply doesn't notice something has been omitted; whereas Freud's case involves someone who knows something has been left out, but doesn't know what. After all, his choosing even to try to quote that Latin line is itself psychologically problematic in a way that corresponds to nothing in the scribe's case. Besides, the sort of experimental evidence that is relevant to, for example, establishing the link between

55. The reference is to Timpanaro, *Freudian Slip.*

smoking and cardiovascular disease and lung cancer is largely *analogical* in nature; tests are conducted on animal subjects to reveal what effects on humans would result if they were subjected to comparable conditions. Similar background knowledge would seem to exist in the case of psychopathology — between patients in treatment and those not (compare Grünbaum, 258–59, who erroneously contrasts neurotics and non-neurotics — as if everyone not in treatment can be assumed to be non-neurotic). So the contrast Grünbaum seeks to draw between the laboratory world of real science and the intraclinical land of unscience ruled by analogy (extrapolation) is greatly exaggerated, since analogies are omnipresent and ineradicable, for example, in his own paradigm case, medical research concerning the effects of smoking.

As for Grünbaum's main argument (192), quoted above, the puzzle about it is what sense Grünbaum is going to be able to give to the premise in it that he is prepared to grant for argument's sake — namely, that the restored awareness of *aliquis* was the cause of the associations leading to the emerging anxiety. Once again, if the only sort of evidence capable of justifying such a claim is assumed to be quasi-epidemiological and experimental, in which analogical inference is supposed to be absent, it is hard to see how it can be given any sense at all. If some other kind of analogical evidence — for example, thematic affinity — is accepted as relevant to the premise, then presumably similar evidence should also be accepted as supporting the conclusion, namely, that the anxiety caused the forgetting of *aliquis,* which Grünbaum denies is supported in that way. The trouble is that we do not learn from Grünbaum what criteria of relevance he is employing when judging the causal relevance of things; is mere thematic affinity never causally relevant, a priori? And what of strong thematic affinity? For one of the most striking things about the young man's free associations in the *aliquis* example is the way *every one* of his associations seemed to allude to his emerging anxiety; whereas far less clear cases are usual — that is, ones in which several of the associations seem to point in other directions, or only uncertainly, to the emerging idea that may have been the cause of the forgetting. Apparently, it is only because Grünbaum denies all evidentiary weight to thematic affinity quite generally, and without any argument at all, that he is able to claim: "The intraclinical testing of the causal assertions made by Freud's specific etiologies of the psychoneuroses . . . is *epistemically quite hopeless!*" (253). For if thematic affinity were to be assumed to have any weight at all, as psychoanalysis assumes, the way would have been made clear for intraclinical testing of psychoanalytic hypotheses, quite continuous with the "time-honored canons of causal inference pioneered by Francis Bacon and John Stuart Mill" (47), which Grünbaum rightly values as essential components of those modes of inquiry that genuinely establish causal relevance.

But without the assumption that thematic affinity has evidentiary weight, it is not only the intraclinical testing of Freud's hypotheses that becomes epistemically hopeless; the interpretation of dreams and slips outside the clinical context also becomes hopeless, as does all cross-cultural testing of psychoanalytic hypotheses. It is remarkable that Grünbaum appears to have entirely neglected to examine any of the distinguished body of material to be found in the work of such psychoanalytically oriented anthropologists as J. W. M. Whiting, M. E. Spiro, and G. Obeyesekere.

These consequences, coupled with the numerous distortions of Freud's texts, as well as the logical confusions integral to those distortions, ought to make us doubt whether the NCT or the Tally Argument are views Freud ever entertained. To regard these claims as having any serious part in interpreting the foundations of psychoanalysis requires in addition such violence to common sense that we must conclude that the foundations of psychoanalysis are entirely different from anything Grünbaum conceives.

But the additional problem mentioned at the start of this chapter is even more troubling. When, as Grünbaum proposes, the testing of psychoanalytic hypotheses is detached from its clinical setting in which resistance and transference phenomena in free association provide the coordinating definitions on the basis of which unconscious ideas and wishes are ascribed, the results are flawed. For then, not only do the hypotheses cease to be genuinely psychoanalytic ones, but, in addition, the hypotheses, in effect, cease to be testable, since the key terms used in formulating those hypotheses are then without meaning. That is, having lost whatever meaning can be gained from the clinical method, new coordinating definitions for *unconscious idea* and *unconscious wish* are needed but have not been provided. It is remarkable that Grünbaum does not address the problem of providing new coordinating definitions for these terms without which the extraclinical testing he proposes is impossible. Without claiming that such new definitions are absolutely impossible, it is nevertheless hard to see what can supply them, and Grünbaum offers no help at all, since he does not discuss the question. The clinical method, it seems, will have to be retained until something better comes along, if it is unconscious ideas and wishes we wish to examine.

Afterword

What has been accomplished in this book? First of all, uncovering the confusion common to the best philosophical criticisms
of psychoanalysis is in itself illuminating, for there can be no doubt
that the systematic avoidance of the subject of resistance and transference phenomena is a major error in *interpreting* Freud, who was
very clear about the central role of such phenomena for psychoanalysis. It would be absurd to fault James, who wrote before psychoanalysis existed, for this confusion, but that Wittgenstein, Mac-
Intyre, and Grünbaum (along with Popper, E. Nagel, and Cioffi) all
fail to recognize the defining role of such phenomena is significant;
many modern philosophers evidently have the same preestablished
intellectual bias that prevents them from seeing what the argument
of psychoanalysis really consists in, and it is a fair bet that if these
thinkers have all stumbled into the same errors of interpretation,
many others, philosophers as well as nonphilosophers have, too. Of
course, it does not help that Freud himself, specifically in his posthypnotic suggestion argument, was capable of distorting his own
ideas about the unconscious.

What becomes of these philosophers' criticisms, given this general tendency to distort in this systematic way? Wittgenstein's worry that psychoanalytic interpretation drives out all other kinds of interpretation, for example, religious interpretation, seems groundless. Of course, Freud himself, atheist that he was, was uninterested in pursuing that road; however, that tells us nothing about the nature of his creation apart from his personality. Not only does the logic of Freud's method of interpreting dreams not require the kind of reductive reading that Wittgenstein (like many readers) assumed, but Freud himself, in responding to the "anagogic" interpretation of dreams proposed by Silberer, shows that it was not nonreductiveness per se that he objected to. Silberer claimed that more serious thoughts, "often of profound import," are revealed in anagogic interpretation, whereas psychoanalytic interpretation usually concerns infantile-sexual meanings.[1] What bothered Freud was Silberer's claim that two different kinds of interpretations are *required,* that they bear a *fixed relation* to each other and are *essentially different,* and that anagogic interpretation requires technical methods that are *different* from Freud's.[2] By contrast, Freud did not object to the idea that "abstract thoughts" might be uncovered in the course of interpreting a dream psychoanalytically.

What about James's idea that conscious ideas that are quickly gone, unattended to, might do the explanatory work that proponents of the unconscious ascribe to unconscious mental activity? For most of the cases in which James tries to effect this replacement, it is possible that he is right; but then there is the case exemplified by the loving feelings in his tenth proof that is not easily dealt with in the prescribed way. Besides, examining less than the full spectrum of cases, that is, leaving out dreams and parapraxes, for example, makes the proposed replacement deceptively easy.

As for MacIntyre's objections that unconscious mental activity, as Freud understands it, is unobservable in some objectionable way, I would reply that it is the concept of unobservability as MacIntyre

1. Freud, *Interpretation of Dreams,* 5:524.
2. Freud, "A Metasychological Supplement to the Theory of Dreams," 14:228n., and *Interpretation of Dreams,* 5:524.

deploys it that is the real source of much of the difficulty he finds. When we realize, in addition, that ideas and wishes are what is unconscious for psychoanalysis, the status of unconscious ideas and wishes does not appear as different from that of conscious ones as MacIntyre imagines.

If this is so, it should make a difference for the sort of argument Grünbaum presents, since he claims that he does not regard psychoanalytic interpretations as unverifiable. But then it is puzzling why the only verifications of psychoanalytic claims that he considers involve tests of efficacy in producing a cure. After all, if the presence in subjects of specific unconscious mental states is testable in some degree not very far removed from that in which the presence of conscious ideas and wishes is testable, it is plausible to expect that causal relations between the unconscious and the conscious mental states could be discovered, independent of any curative power to be found in revealing those unconscious mental states. Yet Grünbaum does not regard any tests of psychoanalytic claims other than longitudinal studies of success in curing psychopathology as having any evidentiary status; not only do those other tests have no probative value, they are not even relevant evidence. Remarkably, Grünbaum does not even argue for this artificial restriction of the range of relevant evidence. Yet without the evidence that can be provided by resistance and transference phenomena, it is hard to see what sense can be given to the reference to unconscious ideas and wishes in interpretations, reference with which Grünbaum claims to have no problem. That is, how are ascriptions of unconscious ideas and wishes to particular subjects meaningful in the absence of the evidence that resistance and transference phenomena provide for such ascriptions? If resistance and transference phenomena are relevant to ascribing unconscious ideas and wishes to subjects, why cannot Freud's etiological hypotheses be tested in any way other than by testing their curative power? Grünbaum does not quarrel, it seems, with the meaningfulness of psychoanalytic ascription of unconscious mental states — but if such phenomena as resistance and transference cannot provide evidence for those ascriptions, what can?

Grünbaum is caught in a dilemma. If he accepts the relevance of resistance and transference phenomena as evidence for ascribing unconscious ideas and wishes to subjects, then Freud's etiological hypotheses ought to be testable apart from tests for success in curing psychopathology. Yet Grünbaum does not regard that as possible, it seems, since he never even considers such alternative tests involving resistance and transference phenomena. If resistance and transference phenomena are not relevant as evidence for such ascriptions, the sense of those ascriptions becomes problematical, for then we do not know what is evidence for those ascriptions, and Grünbaum says nothing about it. After all, the whole sense of ascribing unconscious ideas and wishes to subjects cannot be exhaustively contained in the therapeutic effect of doing so. It is hard to avoid the conclusion that Grünbaum is actually rooted in MacIntyre's position — that is, that Grünbaum, like MacIntyre, must treat the ascription of unconscious ideas and wishes to subjects as scientifically problematic, though he does not say this. For whichever leg of the dilemma he grasps will have an unwelcome consequence. Thus, Grünbaum's proposed longitudinal studies are bound to be problematical; for how can one test for the presence or absence of unconscious ideas and wishes outside the clinical context while holding on to Freud's conception of these ideas and wishes as being what psychoanalytic interpretations are about? In such longitudinal studies, either clinical examination will have to be introduced, or what is being tested for in these studies will be something other than unconscious ideas and wishes, that is, it will be other than what the analysis of resistance and transference phenomena reveal, for Freud.

Thus far, I have presented a mainly negative thesis; that is, I have dwelled upon various errors in interpreting Freud and the objectionable consequences such misinterpretations yield. The results of this extended examination of what I've called the argument of psychoanalysis can be stated more positively. Freud's claim that resistance and transference phenomena are the basis of the psychoanalytic conception of the unconscious implies that what is resisted and transferred are unconscious ideas and wishes; and *this* claim has important implications, if we distinguish ideas and wishes from beliefs and desires, as psychoanalysis, in accordance with ordinary speech, requires. Whereas beliefs and desires are attached to behavior in comparatively straightforward ways, ideas and wishes are not. In contrast to desires and beliefs, it is possible to wish for, or have the idea of, what one knows to be impossible; there are idle wishes, but no idle desires. Wishes need not result in any particular goal-directed behavior—one need not try to obtain what one wishes for, even if one believes it possible to achieve it. So in ascribing ideas and wishes to persons, self-ascription and assent are more centrally controlling criteria than they are in the case of beliefs and desires, where behavior alone will often do. Thus, the difficulty in making sense of the psychoanalytic conception of unconscious mental activity in terms of behavior, apart from resistances and transferences, may result more from the fact that, for psychoanalysis, what is unconscious is ideas and wishes than from the fact that these are supposed to be unconscious mental states. But the difficulty is not as great as may appear, since *conscious* ideas and wishes, about which critics of psychoanalysis do not normally quarrel, share the same supposedly objectionable characteristics.

When these contrasts between ideas and beliefs, wishes and desires are taken seriously, it will cease to seem arbitrary or authoritarian to argue that psychoanalytic inquiry, for example, involving free association, is the favored method for discovering unconscious ideas and wishes in specific cases. For apart from psychoanalysis, we do not have any method at all for systematically exploring the unconscious, that is, for investigating unconscious ideas and wishes. So Freud has not *replaced* anything in our ordinary view of the mind—he has extended it. In short, Freud's method need not be seen as an attempt to engineer the cognitive enthronement of the patient (or, more plausibly, of the analyst) about matters of behavior that previously fell within the purview of common understanding. Instead, his method might more accurately be seen as a well-founded extension of our earlier, vague, and ill-defined intuitions about a part of the mind that hitherto has not been explored systematically at all. Seen that way, psychoanalysis is a major extension of the modernist project of unfolding individual subjectivity independent of traditional assumptions or conventions.

My conclusion, then, is that psychoanalysis is amply equipped to respond to the philosophical criticism that has been mounted against it thus far. No good philosophical arguments against it have been produced, and much empirical evidence supports it. It is no wonder that psychoanalysis has been experienced, from different viewpoints, as a radical shift in human thought, and that many have treated it as an advance in our self-understanding — precisely the extension or unfolding of individual subjectivity that it claims to be.

Appendix: Addendum to Grünbaum

In responding to an article in the *New York Review of Books,* Grünbaum writes that the author, Thomas Nagel,[1] "asserts falsely with David Sachs and Paul Robinson that, in my view, 'therapeutic success... [is] the empirical ground on which Freud's theories must stand or fall.' This account is wrong, if only because I stressed the need for extra-clinical evidence, and even proposed the aforementioned epidemiologic test of Freud's etiology of paranoia."[2] Here, Grünbaum contrasts therapeutic success and his proposed epidemiologic test; the latter he takes to provide extraclinical evidence relevant to Freud's etiology of paranoia, whereas the former does not. The ambiguities implicit in these two claims, that (a) therapeutic success is not extraclinical evidence and (b) the proposed epidemiologic test gives extraclinical evidence (of Freud's etiology of paranoia), need to be explored; because of these ambiguities, (a) and (b) are not stable propositions at all.[3]

1. Nagel, "Freud's Permanent Revolution," 34–38.
2. Grünbaum, "Letter to the Editor," 54. (The works referred to are Sachs, "In Fairness to Freud" and Robinson, *Freud and His Critics.*)
3. I shall ignore here my own disagreement with Grünbaum concerning what social consequences, if any, can be predicted on the basis of Freud's

First of all, one might naively assume, contrary to (a), that therapeutic *success* is observable outside the clinical context and so must be extraclinical evidence; it sounds odd to classify such success as intraclinical evidence. But Grünbaum regards therapeutic success as tainted evidence, since it includes spurious (placebo) results along with genuine outcomes, and thus he excludes it from the category of extraclinical evidence. By itself, however, this argument is a non sequitur; after all, according to Grünbaum, both spurious and genuine successes are observable outside the clinical context, the problem is simply that short of longitudinal studies, we are unable to tell the difference. So instead of (a), the upshot of this argument ought to be that therapeutic success *is* extraclinical evidence, though of different grades of (hard to distinguish) reliability.

However, it is also possible to assert (a) as a tautology, meaning something like "success *resulting from* clinical effort is not evidence that results *independent of* clinical effort." Two consequences of treating (a) as a tautology need to be emphasized. One is that when so treated, the therapeutic success in question cannot be extraclinical evidence even after longitudinal studies with experimental controls have confirmed the genuineness of that therapeutic success. The second consequence is that what Grünbaum means by "therapeutic success" will be different from what Nagel, Sachs, and Robinson mean by it in the account of his views that he is intent on refuting, as we shall see.

Pretty clearly, what Grünbaum means by "success" in "therapeutic success" is not the standard meaning, if (a) is to be assumed true; for, in Grünbaum's view, therapeutic success encompasses both genuine and illusory cases of success. It is as if someone were to include under the heading "Picasso's Paintings" all the counterfeits along with the genuine ones. What Grünbaum means is really properly expressed as "therapeutic 'success'" — that is with ironic quotation marks around the word *success*.

What makes the results of the epidemiologic test (what I called the social test) extraclinical evidence for Grünbaum, seems to be the fact that, according to him, the anticipated reduction (or lack of it) in the incidence of paranoia is not produced by clinical means; by contrast, therapeutic "suc-

---

etiology of paranoia once taboos on homosexuality are lifted; in other words, I shall assume for the sake of argument that Grünbaum is right that Freud's etiology predicts that when social taboos on homosexuality are lifted, the incidence of paranoia will decline.

cess," for him, results from clinical endeavor and therefore might be a place-bo effect.[4] So Grünbaum does seem to mean (a) in its tautological sense.

Now without questioning the truth of (a), there is an even more important ambiguity in it that must be noted; for *therapeutic* can mean either (1) having healing or curative powers or (2) the medical treatment of disease. When Grünbaum rejects the quoted claim ascribed to him (that is, the claim that "therapeutic success is the ground on which Freud's theories must stand or fall"),[5] he changes the sense of the term *therapeutic* from (1) to (2), although that claim obviously intended (1), since in sense (1), Grünbaum's proposed epidemiologic test *is* a test of therapeutic success. For in that test, according to Grünbaum, the incidence of a pathological state — paranoia — will decline, if Freud's etiology is correct. That no therapists' activities are involved in producing this result is irrelevant to whether it is a case of therapeutic success, in sense (1). It would be an arbitrary restriction on the meaning of therapeutic to require that therapeutic success must be the result of some therapist's efforts. A thing is therapeutic, in sense (1), if it has healing or curative powers and therefore may have therapeutic powers without being administered or prescribed by a therapist, as is illustrated by one of the examples the *Oxford English Dictionary* gives under "therapeutic" from 1842: "cold water has long been known as a therapeutic." So Grünbaum's epidemiologic test results in therapeutic success in sense (1) if Freud's etiology is correct. Since therapeutic success is ambiguous, capable of meaning (1) or (2), there is of course no use in claiming that one or the other is the correct sense. Certainly, it is a simple matter to circumvent this purely verbal issue, for the essential point is that Grünbaum does hold that removal of, or reduction in, pathology, without regard to what sort of effort produced it, is the empirical ground on which Freud's theories must stand or fall, and his proposed epidemiologic test is no exception to that claim.[6] So if (a) is meant

---

4. It is odd that Grünbaum does not seem to be bothered by the possibility of a placebo effect distorting the results of his proposed epidemiologic test comparable to that possibility in regard to therapeutic success.

5. This is the same claim that I labeled (B) in chapter 4.

6. I have not discussed here, as Grünbaum does not, the whole question of whether it is possible to determine whether the incidence of paranoia has declined in his epidemiologic test entirely apart from clinical inquiry; certainly, if this could not be determined without clinical inquiry, Grünbaum's views would be put in question.

tautologically when Grünbaum invokes it as an expression of his views, (a) also then employs therapeutic success in a different sense from that employed in the assertion by Nagel, Sachs, and Robinson that Grünbaum seeks to refute by invoking (a). The sense in which their assertion uses therapeutic success is one in which (a) is simply false, since at least one case of therapeutic success — that is, the result of the epidemiologic test — is extraclinical evidence. But a claim cannot be refuted simply by altering its sense and then disproving the new claim that results.

What Grünbaum does not even consider is the possibility of evidence for etiological claims of an entirely different kind from removal of, or reduction in, pathology, although Freud presents it right from the start — for example, in the extended analogy between "traumatic" hysteria and common hysteria,[7] where the causal relation between psychical trauma and symptom is supposed to be established before any claims are made concerning the therapeutic efficacy of recollection and abreaction.

The same point concerning Grünbaum's blind spot about the kinds of evidence Freud offers needs to be made when Grünbaum claims, "It is incontestable that Freud offered a *therapeutic* justification for the etiologic probativeness he attributed to his method of free association" and refers to the *Interpretation of Dreams* (5:528) in support. What Freud actually says there is very far from a therapeutic justification for the etiologic probativeness of free association, regardless of which sense of therapeutic is assumed. First of all, the subject under discussion for Freud is the use of free association applied to dreams, where, of course, there is no question of therapeutic justification — with very rare exceptions, dreams are not symptoms to be (1) healed or cured or (2) treated medically at all. To justify the use of free association in interpreting dreams, Freud appeals first to "the surprising connections with other elements of the dream which emerge in the course of our pursuing a single one of its ideas, and to the improbability that anything which gives such an exhaustive account of the dream could have been arrived at except by following up psychical connections which had already been laid down." Obviously, no therapeutic justification is involved here; the only result sought or achieved in employing free association in regard to a dream is the elucidation of the meaning of the dream. Freud goes on, adding as a separate, and subordinate, point: "We might also point out in our defence that our procedure in interpreting dreams is identical with the procedure by which we resolve hysterical symptoms; and there the correct-

7. Freud, *Studies on Hysteria*, 2:4–6.

ness of our method is warranted by the coincident emergence and disappearance of the symptoms, or, to use a simile, the assertions made in the text are borne out by the accompanying illustrations."[8] Here, in the case of hysterical symptoms, it is the fact that the symptom emerges from *the same* point whose uncovering leads to its disappearance that warrants free association's claim to reveal causes. But if the points of emergence and disappearance were not the same, even given therapeutic success, free association's claim to reveal causes in the case of hysterical symptoms would not be warranted. That is, in the case of such symptoms, if we suppose that free association to something other than the point of emergence — for example, to some ideal state, say, freedom from the symptom, can cause the symptom to disappear — then free association's claim to reveal causes would not be supported, for Freud. Yet in this hypothetical case, free association results in therapeutic success. So it is only in a Pickwickian sense that one can speak of Freud offering a therapeutic justification for the etiologic probativeness of free association, since it is not the therapeutic success per se that is evidence of free association's etiologic probativeness. The cause of the symptom's emergence is taken to be established independent of the therapeutic success that can then be produced based on it; but, for Freud, that success itself provides further evidence warranting free association's claim to etiologic probativeness. Thus, there is both a "text," that is, a causal account of the symptom, and supporting "illustrations," that is, symptom removal.

I conclude that Grünbaum does not support his claim that Freud offered a therapeutic justification for the etiologic probativeness he attributed to free association; and we have already seen that Grünbaum does not refute the claim that he himself is committed to the view that therapeutic success is the empirical ground on which Freud's theories must stand or fall, that is, he is committed to claim (B), as I demonstrated in the preceding chapter.

8. Freud, *Interpretation of Dreams*, 5:528.

References

Achinstein, P. (1970). "The Problem of Theoretical Terms." In *Readings in the Philosophy of Science,* edited by B. A. Brody, 234–50. Englewood Cliffs, N.J.: Prentice-Hall. (Originally in *American Philosophical Quarterly* 2, no. 3 [July 1965]: 193–203).

Alston, W. (1967). "Psychoanalytic Theories, Logical Status of." In *The Encyclopedia of Philosophy,* edited by P. Edwards, 6:512–16. New York: Macmillan.

Balint, M. (1965). *Primary Love and Psycho-analytic Technique.* New York: Liveright.

Bouveresse, J. (1995). *Wittgenstein Reads Freud: The Myth of the Unconscious.* Translated by C. Cosman. Princeton, N.J.: Princeton University Press.

Cavell, M. (1993). *The Psychoanalytic Mind: From Freud to Philosophy.* Cambridge, Mass.: Harvard University Press.

Cioffi, F. (1969). "Wittgenstein's Freud." In *Studies in the Philosophy of Wittgenstein,* edited by P. Winch, 184–210. London: Routledge.

———. (1970). "Freud and the Idea of a Pseudo-Science." In *Explanation in the Behavioural Sciences,* edited by R. Borger and F. Cioffi, 471–98. Cambridge: Cambridge University Press.

References

Domhoff, G. W. (1985). *The Mystique of Dreams*. Berkeley: University of California Press.

Drury, M. (1967). Symposium contribution in *Ludwig Wittgenstein: The Man and His Philosophy*, edited by K. T. Fann. New York: Dell.

Erdelyi, M. H. (1985). *Psychoanalysis: Freud's Cognitive Psychology*. New York: W. H. Freeman.

Erikson, Erik H. (1954). "The Dream Specimen of Psychoanalysis." *Journal of the American Psychoanalytic Association* 2:5–56.

———. (1964). "The Nature of Clinical Evidence." In *Insight and Responsibility*. New York: Norton.

Fisher, S., and Greenberg, R. P. (1977). *The Scientific Credibility of Freud's Theories and Therapy*. New York: Basic Books.

Freud, S. (1953–74). *The Standard Edition of the Complete Psychological Works*. Edited and translated by J. Strachey. 24 volumes. London: Hogarth. The following references to this edition (*S.E.*) include volume and, when applicable, pages.

———. (1893). "On the Psychical Mechanism of Hysterical Phenomena: A Lecture." *S.E.* 3:27–39.

———. (1894). "The Neuro-Psychoses of Defence." *S.E.* 3:45–61.

———. (1895 [1894]). "On the Grounds for Detaching a Particular Syndrome from Neurasthenia under the Description 'Anxiety Neurosis.'" *S.E.* 3:90–115.

———. (1895). *Studies on Hysteria,* by J. Breuer and S. Freud. *S.E.* 2.

———. (1896). "Further Remarks on the Neuro-Psychoses of Defence." *S.E.* 3:157–85.

———. (1896). "The Aetiology of Hysteria." *S.E.* 3:191–221.

———. (1900). *The Interpretation of Dreams. S.E.* 4–5.

———. (1901). *The Psychopathology of Everyday Life. S.E.* 6.

———. (1905). *Jokes and Their Relation to the Unconscious. S.E.* 8.

———. (1905). *Three Essays on the Theory of Sexuality. S.E.* 7:130–243.

———. (1905). "Fragment of an Analysis of a Case of Hysteria." *S.E.* 7:7–122.

———. (1908). "'Civilized' Sexual Morality and Modern Nervous Illness." *S.E.* 9:181–204.

———. (1909). "Analysis of a Phobia in a Five-Year-Old Boy." *S.E.* 10:5–149.

———. (1910). "The Future Prospects of Psycho-Analytic Therapy." *S.E.* 11:141–51.

———. (1911). "Psycho-Analytic Notes on an Autobiographical Account of a Case of Paranoia (Dementia Paranoides)." *S.E.* 12:9–82.

———. (1912). "The Dynamics of Transference." *S.E.* 12:97–108.

———. (1912). "A Note on the Unconscious in Psycho-Analysis." *S.E.* 12: 255–66.

———. (1913 [1912–1913]). *Totem and Taboo. S.E.* 13:xii–172.

———. (1914). *On the History of the Psycho-Analytic Movement. S.E.* 14: 7–66.

———. (1914). "On Narcissism: An Introduction." *S.E.* 14:73–102.

———. (1915 [1914]). "Observations on Transference-Love." *S.E.* 12:157–73.

———. (1915). "Repression." *S.E.* 14: 143–158.

———. (1915). "The Unconscious." *S.E.* 14:159–215.

———. (1915). "A Case of Paranoia Running Counter to the Psycho-Analytic Theory of the Disease." *S.E.* 14:261–72.

———. (1916–17 [1915–17]). *Introductory Lectures on Psycho-Analysis. S.E.* 15–16.

———. (1917 [1915]). "A Metapsychological Supplement to the Theory of Dreams." *S.E.* 14:222–35.

———. (1917 [1915]). "Mourning and Melancholia." *S.E.* 14:243–58.

———. (1918 [1914]). "From the History of an Infantile Neurosis." *S.E.* 17:7–122.

———. (1919). "Preface to Reik's *Ritual: Psycho-Analytic Studies. S.E.* 17: 257–63.

———. (1922). "Some Neurotic Mechanisms in Jealousy, Paranoia and Homosexuality." *S.E.* 18:221–32.

———. (1923). "Two Encyclopedia Articles." *S.E.* 18:235–59.

———. (1923). *The Ego and the Id. S.E.* 19:1–66.

———. (1926). *The Question of Lay Analysis. S.E.* 20:177–258.

———. (1933). *New Introductory Lectures on Psycho-Analysis. S.E.* 22.

———. (1937). "Analysis Terminable and Interminable." *S.E.* 23:209–53.

———. (1937). "Constructions in Analysis." *S.E.* 23:255–69.

———. (1940 [1938]). *An Outline of Psycho-Analysis. S.E.* 23:139–207.

———. (1940 [1938]). "Some Elementary Lessons in Psycho-Analysis." *S.E.* 23:279–86.

———. (1985). *The Complete Letters of Sigmund Freud to Wilhelm Fliess (1887–1904).* Edited and translated by J. Masson. Cambridge, Mass.: Harvard University Press.

References

Frieden, K. (1990). *Freud's Dream of Interpretation.* Albany: State University Press of New York.

Gould, S. J. (1977). "Darwin's Untimely Burial." In *Ever Since Darwin,* 39–45. New York: Norton.

Grünbaum, A. (1984). *The Foundations of Psychoanalysis: A Philosophical Critique.* Berkeley: University of California Press.

———. (1994). "Letter to the Editor," *New York Review of Books* 41, no. 14 (August 11): 54–55.

Guttman, A., editor (1984). *The Concordance to the Standard Edition of the Complete Psychological Works of Sigmund Freud.* New York: International Universities Press.

Hempel, C. (1965 [1945]). "Studies in the Logic of Confirmation." In *Aspects of Scientific Explanation,* 3–51. New York: The Free Press.

———. (1965 [1958]). "The Theoretician's Dilemma: A Study in the Logic of Theory Construction." In *Aspects of Scientific Explanation,* 173–226. New York: The Free Press.

James, W. (1950 [1890]). *The Principles of Psychology.* 2 vols. Reprint, New York: Dover.

Jones, E. (1953). *The Life and Work of Sigmund Freud.* 3 vols. New York: Basic Books.

Jung, C. (1938). *Psychology and Religion.* New Haven: Yale University Press.

Kenny, A. (1963). *Action, Emotion and Will.* London: Routledge.

Kraus, K. (1954). *Werke,* vol. 3. Edited by Heinrich Fischer. 14 vols. Munich: Kosel Verlag.

Laplanche, J., and Pontalis, J.-B. (1973). *The Language of Psychoanalysis.* Translated by D. Nicholson-Smith from 1967 French original. New York: Norton.

Levy, D. (1983a). "Post-Hypnotic Suggestion and the Existence of Unconscious Mental Activity." *Analysis* 43, no. 4 (October): 184–89.

———. (1983b). "Wittgenstein on the Form of Psychoanalytic Interpretation." *International Review of Psycho-Analysis* 10:105–9.

———. (1987). Review of Grünbaum's *The Foundations of Psychoanalysis: A Philosophical Critique.* *PsychCritique* 2:329–36.

———. (1988). "Grünbaum's Freud." *Inquiry* 31:193–215.

Lindzey, G. (1958). "The Assessment of Human Motives." In *The Assessment of Human Motives,* edited by G. Lindzey. New York: Holt, Rinehart and Winston.

McGuinness, B. (1982). "Freud and Wittgenstein". In *Wittgenstein and His Times*, editor B. McGuinness. Oxford: Blackwell.

MacIntyre, A. (1958). *The Unconscious: A Conceptual Study*. London: Routledge.

Madison, P. (1961). *Freud's Concept of Repression and Defense, Its Theoretical and Observational Language*. Minneapolis: University of Minnesota Press.

Malcolm, N. (1958). *Ludwig Wittgenstein: A Memoir; with a Biographical Sketch by Georg Henrik von Wright*. London: Oxford University Press.

Moore, B. E., and Fine, B. D., editors. (1990). *Psychoanalytic Terms and Concepts*. New Haven: Yale University Press and the American Psychoanalytic Association.

Moore, G. E. (1962). "Wittgenstein's Lectures in 1930–33." *Philosophical Papers*. New York: Collier Books. (First published in *Mind* 63 [1954] and 64 [1955].)

Nagel, E. (1959). "Methodological Issues in Psychoanalytic Theory." In *Psychoanalysis, Scientific Method and Philosophy*, edited by S. Hook. New York: New York University Press.

Nagel, T. (1994). "Freud's Permanent Revolution." *New York Review of Books* 41, no. 9 (May 12): 34–38.

Newton, I. (1931 [1730]). *Opticks*. 4th ed. Reprint, New York: McGraw-Hill.

Obeyesekere, G. (1990). *The Work of Culture*. Chicago: University of Chicago Press.

Popper, K. (1962). *Conjectures and Refutations*. New York: Basic Books.

Potter, S. (1951). *Lifemanship*. New York: Henry Holt & Company.

Putnam, H. (1979). "What Theories Are Not." *Philosophical Papers*, vol. 1, 2d ed. Cambridge: Cambridge University Press.

Reber, A. (1985). *The Penguin Dictionary of Psychology*. Harmondsworth: Penguin Books.

Robinson, P. (1993). *Freud and His Critics*. Berkeley: University of California Press.

Sachs, D. (1989). "In Fairness to Freud: A Critical Notice of *The Foundations of Psychoanalysis* by Adolf Grünbaum." *Philosophical Review* 98: 349–78.

Shapere, D. (1969). "Notes Toward a Post-Positivistic Interpretation of Science." In *The Legacy of Logical Positivism*, edited by P. Achinstein and S. Barker. Baltimore: Johns Hopkins University Press.

References

Spiro, M. (1982). *Oedipus in the Trobriands*. Chicago: University of Chicago Press.

Tedlock, B. editor. (1992). *Dreaming: Anthropological and Psychological Interpretations*. Santa Fe, N.M.: School of American Research Press.

Timpanaro, S. (1976). *The Freudian Slip*. Translated by K. Soper. Atlantic Highlands, N.J.: Humanities Press.

Westfall, R. S. (1962). "The Development of Newton's Theory of Color." *Isis* 53, pt. 3, no. 173, 339–58.

Whiting, J. W. M. (1961). "Socialization Process and Personality." In *Psychological Anthropology*, edited by F. L. K. Hsu. Homewood, Ill.: Dorsey Press.

Wisdom, J. O. (1956–57). "Psycho-analytic Technology." *British Journal for the Philosophy of Science* 7:13–28.

———. (1966). "Testing a Psycho-Analytic Interpretation." *Ratio* 8:55–76.

Wittgenstein, L. (1953). *Philosophical Investigations*. Translated by G. Anscombe. Edited by G. Anscombe and R. Rhees. Oxford: Blackwell.

———. (1958). *The Blue and Brown Books*. Oxford: Blackwell. First dictated in 1933–34.

———. (1961). *Tractatus Logico-Philosophicus*. New English translation by D. F. Pears and B. F. McGuinness of 1918 original. London: Routledge.

———. (1966). *Lectures and Conversations on Aesthetics, Psychology and Religious Belief*. Edited by Cyril Barrett. Berkeley: University of California Press.

———. (1979). *Wittgenstein's Lectures, Cambridge, 1932–1935: From the Notes of Alice Ambrose and Margaret MacDonald*. Edited by A. Ambrose. Chicago: University of Chicago Press.

———. (1980). *Culture and Value* (Vermischte Bemerkungen). Edited by G. H. von Wright. Translated by P. Winch. Chicago: University of Chicago Press.

Wollheim, R. (1971). *Sigmund Freud*. New York: Viking Press.

———. (1984). *The Thread of Life*. Cambridge, Mass.: Harvard University Press.

Index